L
Memory Jogger
for Healthcare

Richard L. MacInnes
Net Results, Inc.

Mark L. Dean PhD
Dean & Associates, LLC

First Edition | A GOAL/QPC Publication

MEMORY JOGGER
We remember the tools for you

The Lean Memory Jogger™ for Healthcare

Development Team

Authors:	Richard L. MacInnes
	Mark L. Dean PhD
Project Management:	Daniel Griffiths
	Susan Griebel
Designer:	Janet MacCausland
Project Editor:	nSight, Inc.

Publication Review Team

Pat Duce, RN

Elisabeth Keim, Integrated Quality Resources, LLC

Scott D Kuiper MD, Louisville Orthopedic Clinic

GOAL/QPC | Memory Jogger
8E Industrial Way, Suite 3, Salem, NH 03079
800.643.4316 or 603.893.1944
service@goalqpc.com
MemoryJogger.org

Printed in the United States of America
ISBN: 978-1-57681-152-8

10   9   8   7   6   5   4   3   2

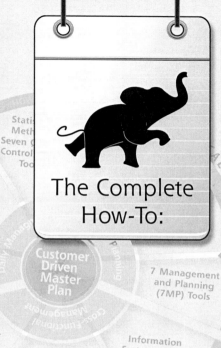

Statistical
Methods
Seven QC
Control
Tools

Continuous
Improvement
and
Standardization

...nd
...nt

Customer/Supplier
Executive
...ms

Daily Management

Planning

Cross-Functional
Management

Customer
Driven
Master
Plan

The Complete
How-To:

7 Management
and Planning
(7MP) Tools

Information
Systems/Audit
Tools

Quality Systems
Quality Function
Deployment (QFD)

VERTICAL ALIGNMENT

HORIZONTAL INTEGRATION

How to Use This Pocket Guide

The Lean Memory Jogger™ for Healthcare is designed for you to use as a convenient and quick reference guide on the job or on the go. Our "*What is it?*" "*Why use it?*" and "*How do I do it?*" format is crucial for understanding and retention of the tools. Put your finger on any individual tool within seconds! Use this guide as part of a self-study program or as a reference before, during, and after your training to learn the different types of tools and their uses.

Our GOAL/QPC on-site workshops offer the highest rate of educational retention. Host a workshop for hands-on practice, today!

GOAL/QPC

7 Management & Planning Tools—On-site Workshop

Using Data for Fact-Based Decision Making, A 2-Day Training Workshop. *Available as Train-the-Trainer.*

Improve your company's overall performance through effective planning, decision making, and breakthrough thinking. Gain support for complex decision making, identifying key issues, and discover causes of persistent problems. Deliver bottom-line results or solutions to problems and assist in personnel selection, performance analysis, conflict resolution, and strategic planning.

GOAL/QPC
Quality

7 Quality Control Tools—On-site Workshop

A 2-Day Training Workshop. *Available as Train-the-Trainer.*

This workshop will assist you in evaluating cycle time, costs, and other results related to your daily work, as well as provide tools to help improve product quality, productivity, and process management.

Available digitally on MemoryJogger.org

Most of our Memory Joggers are available as digital eBooks. You can use eBooks on your PC or Mac, as well as your eReaders. Purchasing in multiple quantities is an excellent way to train across corporate locations or all in the same meeting room.

Make It Your Own

Take any Memory Jogger and apply your company's own personal style. Customization allows you to creatively combine the contents of GOAL/QPC products with your own documents and training materials. We can deliver to digital eBook or as a print version.

See **MemoryJogger.org/custom**

Know the Tool You Need?

Find it by using the:

Table of contents. Tools, techniques, the case study—it's in alphabetical order.

Solid tab. Look for the blue or black solid box at the bottom of the first page of each new section.

How to Use the Book

This book will explain what you need to know to apply lean methods to a Healthcare Enterprise's processes and workplace. The specific information you will learn includes the following:

○ Concepts and definitions you need to know

○ Skills you need to develop

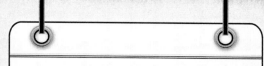

- Tools you need to use
- Steps you need to take

This information will help you and your team work together systematically toward your lean Healthcare Enterprise goals.

This *Lean Memory Jogger™ for Healthcare* (LMJH) is designed to assist you in the application of specific lean methodologies. The LMJH works in combination with *The Lean Healthcare Implementer's Field Book*, the purpose of which is to provide essential insight for implementing a *Lean Transformation* within your Healthcare Enterprise.

Acknowledgements

Our sincere thanks to the people and organizations who reviewed *The Lean Memory Jogger™ for Healthcare* and offered suggestions and encouragement. Their participation in the development process assured us that the approach and methods described in this book are relevant and appropriate for all associates to use in their quest to achieve "Perfect Care"— the ultimate lean goal.

Pat Duce, *RN*

Elisabeth Keim,
Integrated Quality Resources, LLC

Scott D Kuiper MD,
Louisville Orthopedic Clinic

Table of Contents

Introduction

The Lean Healthcare Enterprise

Providers of healthcare services, e.g., doctor offices, clinics, surgical centers, nursing homes, and hospitals, recognize the need for ongoing improvement in processes and resources. The goal of efficiently and effectively restoring and managing patient health while preventing unexpected loss of life is the paramount lean goal of lean methodologies. To be clear, *lean is not the healing process; it is the process for healing processes.*

To be the best health system, lean organizations strive to match medical services to patient needs—exactly as demanded and with no waste in effort or resources. We call this *Perfect Care.*

The Lean Goal Is Simply Perfection

One word sums up the goal of Lean—*Perfection*. In order to maximize the benefits of lean methodologies you must be able to

o imagine perfection;

o pursue perfection;

o deliver perfection; and

o perfect perfection.

Healthcare leadership driven to excellence understands that dedicated resources must work *on* the system with the goal of perfecting the throughputs, processes, and resources of those who work *in* the system. Imagining and defining the *future perfect objective* of these improvement efforts is an essential component of *Lean Transformation* activities—with the ultimate *future perfect objective* of achieving *Perfect Care*.

What We Mean by *Perfect Care*

To be the best health system, lean organizations strive to match medical services to patient needs—exactly as demanded with no waste in effort or resources. We call this *Perfect Care*.

Lean methodologies strive for *Perfect Care* by designing healthcare processes that efficiently and effectively treat symptoms, restore patient health, and prevent unexpected loss of life, given the constraint of available resources. Lean is foremost a resource deployment, optimization, and waste elimination strategy—not a patient medical treatment strategy.

Resources include such things as medical staff, diagnostic technology, supplies, healthcare facilities, special equipment, and medical protocols—all supplies that are required to meet demand *exactly*.

Imagine an Emergency Department (ED) where all patients seeking treatment (demand) are met with the exact resources (supply) required to respond to them instantaneously and meet their needs exactly—no more, no less. Imagine this same objective accomplished across outpatient and inpatient care, clinical care, and managed care services. *Perfect Care* is the *future perfect objective* that provides direction to all lean initiatives.

What Does Lean Process Perfection Look Like?

What is the lean *future perfect objective* in its universal form? **Answer:**

> ➡ Instantaneous satisfaction of a demand, in the form, time, place, cost, and experience desired by the customer; doing so with the optimal economic combination and sequencing of resources at any given moment in time.

We call this definition the *Lean Perfection Standard*. Impossible to achieve, you may say. Yes, but it is directionally correct. It is against this *Lean Perfection Standard* that all healthcare services, processes, and resource investment decisions should be "measured twice and cut once."

The information contained herein is our effort at providing necessary insight to make what may appear to be an intangible lean *future perfect objective* tangible.

Converting Lean Insight into Lean Results

To be successful in the application of lean methods, consider these insights gained from real-world experience.

o Lean is more than waste elimination or just-in-time (JIT); it attempts to match supply to demand—exactly.

o Lean does not rush to organize work areas and produce standards; rather, it continually strives to optimize and manage both processes and requisite resources to meet customer[1] demand.

o Lean complements and integrates with such initiatives as Six Sigma, Total Quality Management (TQM), Change Management, Organizational Redesign, Business Process Reengineering (BPR), but it is distinct from these initiatives.

o Lean is an adaptive process that is constantly sensing changes in demand requirements and realigning supply capabilities.

o Lean methodology is composed of multiple tools, which are themselves constantly changing to reflect advancements in analysis techniques and interpretation.

Insight alone does not guarantee success. If it did, then the numerous "certified" improvement experts in the healthcare community would certainly have more to show for their wisdom. The key is to translate insight into tangible progress toward *Perfect Care*. To that end, this *Lean Memory Jogger™ for Healthcare* (LMJH) is supplemented by the *Lean Healthcare*

Implementer's Field Book (LHIFB), the purpose of which is to provide essential insight for implementing a *Lean Transformation* within your Healthcare Enterprise. The *Lean Transformation Roadmap* shown in Figure I-1 is fully explained in the LHIFB, providing necessary guidance for those leading the *Lean Transformation*.

What Do We Mean When We Say "Healing Pathway" vs. "Business Pathway"?

Healing Pathways are the *core* clinical processes that impact the ability to diagnose, treat, and provide ongoing care. There are many versions of the Healing Pathway depending on the services offered by the Healthcare Enterprise. From the patient's perspective the Healing Pathways matter most, so they should also matter most to you.

Business Pathways can be integral to core Healing Pathways as well as enabling. Examples include transactions that support patient check-in, insurance validation and approvals, inpatient services, and outpatient services. The core Healing Pathways depend on these enabling Business Pathways. The interdependence between Healing and Business Pathways is real and necessary, and significantly impacts the Healthcare Enterprise's ability to deliver patient care.

(Endnotes)

1 The term "customer" is used to represent a patient, a recipient of a process throughput, or both.

2 The term "service" is used to represent both products and services.

Lean Transformation Roadmap

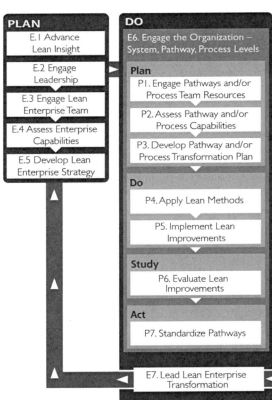

Figure 1-1—Lean Transformation Roadmap

Plan - Do - Study - Act (PDSA)

STUDY
- E8. Evaluate Lean Transformation Progress
- E9. Evaluate Lean Transformation Results
- E9. Evaluate Lean Transformation Capabilities

ACT
- E11. Recognize Lean Transformation Efforts and Results
- E12. Improve Lean Transformation Methodologies
- E13. Improve Lean Transformation Management Capabilities

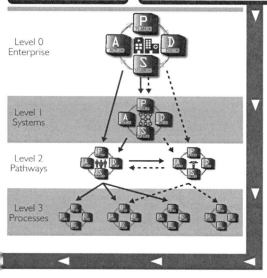

Level 0 Enterprise

Level 1 Systems

Level 2 Pathways

Level 3 Processes

What Do We Mean When We Say "Healthcare System Hierarchy"?

The Healthcare System Hierarchy shown in Figure I-2 will be used to describe the cascading relationships between Level 0 – Healthcare Enterprise, Level 1 – Systems, Level 2 – Pathways, Level 3 – Processes, and Level 4 – Activities.

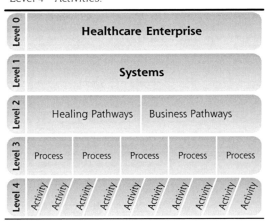

Figure I-2—Healthcare System Hierarchy

Level 0 – Enterprise spans the entirety of healthcare services and operations, including external suppliers and service providers.

Level 1 – System includes enterprise-wide systems, such as information systems, compliance systems, power supply systems, and so on.

Level 2 – Healing Pathways includes specific value streams that impact the clinical processes that comprise the Healing Pathways.

Level 2 – Business Pathways includes specific nonclinical processes that execute vital business and operational activities to ensure organizational sustainability, ultimately enabling the Healing Pathways.

Level 3 – Process includes processes that comprise either Healing and Business Pathways or their interaction. It is at the process level that tangible transformation efforts are made.

What Do We Mean When We Say "Resources"?

The term "resource" or "resources" is used throughout this book to refer to people, protocols, special equipment, information technology, medical supplies, facilities, etc.—System, Pathway, and Process elements necessary to achieve *Perfect Care*. As one explores Levels 0 through 4 per Figure I-2, note how resource capabilities are combined to produce an output is critical to achieving lean objectives. For example, in an emergency care situation, resources may include human cognitive skills needed to ascertain and treat the patient's condition, patient vital signs, IV fluids, portable resuscitation equipment, an ambulance, and so on.

Case Report: Healing U's Lean Transformation

Throughout this text we have simplified and generalized lean healthcare transformational examples under the banner of the Healing U Medical Center (Healing U). Healing U is a small community acute care system consisting of a main campus and two Ambulatory Surgery Centers (ASC). The main campus is a Level One Trauma Center, with a full range of specialists performing services every day, all year. Each ASC operates an Emergency Department (ED) and provides outpatient surgery and diagnostic services.

What Do We Mean When We Say "Lean Methods"?

This Memory Jogger will address lean methodologies organized in a manner typical of how they are used in transforming specific processes and workplaces to achieve lean goals. Lean methods to be discussed include the following.

- ○ Lean Enterprise Goals
- ○ Enterprise Mapping
- ○ Value Stream Mapping
- ○ Service Blueprinting
- ○ Continuous Flow
- ○ Queuing Strategies
- ○ Visual Management
- ○ Error Proofing
- ○ Quick Changeover
- ○ Kanban Systems
- ○ Total Productive Maintenance
- ○ Standard Operations
- ○ Lean Metrics

Chapter ONE

THE LEAN OBJECTIVE

Lean is an overarching philosophy with supporting methodologies for moving a Healthcare Enterprise toward *Perfect Care*. It does so through elimination of waste and non-value-adding activities found in the mismatch of supply to demand and the poor application of resources for achieving *Perfect Care*.

Lean serves as an umbrella strategy, working in concert with other initiatives, e.g., Six Sigma, TQM, etc., to delight customers, empower employees, reengineer processes, and reduce variation, while delivering successful business results to stakeholders. As an implementer of the lean philosophy, your objective is not to compete with other improvement initiatives. Your objective is to focus all improvement efforts toward envisioning, pursuing, delivering, and perfecting supply to match customer demand— exactly. The *Lean Perfection Standard* is the

- Instantaneous satisfaction of a demand in the form, time, place, cost, and experience expected by the customer; doing so with the optimal economic combination and sequencing of resources at any given moment in time.

Lean Value Stream Goals

Value Stream Goals are constructed to guide analysis of customer demand, supply of healthcare services, and resource optimization. Value stream is defined as "a systematic series of activities that produce a defined output." Value Stream Goals are organized in a proven sequence for matching medical services to patient needs. As lean practitioners we recommend that you reflect on these goals, their meaning, how they interact with each other, and why they are sequenced in such a manner. This is insight that matters.

The Value Stream Goals are

- Define Demand;
- Extend Demand Lead Time;
- Match Supply to Demand;
- Eliminate Waste;
- Reduce Supply Lead Time; and
- Reduce Total Costs.

Goal #1: Define Demand

> Lean Perfection Standard: "Instantaneous satisfaction of demand in the form, time, place, cost, and experience expected by the customer..."

It cannot be stated more emphatically that **demand belongs to the customer**[1], with the primary customer being the **patient**. Healthcare providers must clearly define customer demand and thus the demand for their services in a field where customer demand for services is often sporadic, infrequent, and lacking sufficient data to predict it reliably. As a lean practitioner you must not bypass or give insufficient attention to Value Stream Goal #1.

Form, time, place, cost, and experience are essential dimensions of a customer's demand for healthcare services[2]. **Form** is the inherent *design features* of the service. **Time** is the ability to deliver the service at the *time* the customer requires. The **place** dimension is the ability to perform a service at a *location* that the customer can access. **Cost** is the price at which the customer can afford the provided service. Last, **experience** reflects the nature of the interaction the customer has with the healthcare provider throughout all phases of service delivery. The form, time, place, cost, and experience dimensions of demand serve as the drivers for service design and value stream optimization.

Healing Pathways and Business Pathways must be designed to deliver services to match demand. Healing Pathway demand is created and owned by the patient, the BIG D. Business Pathway demand is defined by the service or product requirements of the healthcare enterprise, the small *d*. Every small *d* should have a direct or indirect relationship to the patient's BIG D. If it does not, this is a significant indicator of waste.

Goal #2: Extend Demand Lead Time

⫲ Lean Perfection Standard: "Instantaneous satisfaction of demand . . ."

Experience suggests that to meet customer demand, supply resources must be made available—but which resources should be available, and in what quantity? How long should they be waiting for customer demand to occur? Extending demand lead time requires that one ascertain real demand for both BIG D and small *d* as early as possible. Imagine the value of knowing, at this very instant, that a patient is going to need respiratory care at 3 P.M. this Tuesday and again at 1 A.M. this Friday. How would that help you make the right resources available to meet this demand? Having this insight is the purpose of Goal #2.

Extending demand lead time improves the organization's capabilities to sense real and emerging demand at the earliest possible moment in time. In so doing, the greatest possible demand lead time is provided to the Healthcare Enterprise for making right resources available at the right time.

As you analyze ways to extend demand lead time, attempt to expose false or heightened notions of demand. For example, when is the report really needed? When do expedited shipments of medical supplies really get used? Is the patient really sick?

Goal #3: Match Supply to Demand

> ⌗ Lean Perfection Standard: ". . . doing so with the optimal economic combination and sequencing of resources at any given moment in time."

By *supply* we mean the coordinated system of organizations and their resources—people, processes, information, equipment, and methods—required to deliver healthcare services to patients. Supply matched to demand from a *Perfect Care* perspective requires the necessary healthcare resources to be available at the exact time of patient need.

Matching supply to demand invariably requires changing resource timing and quantity, modifying hours of operations, opening or closing service locations, and so on to ensure better alignment of supply of services to the real demands of patients at the exact time of need. Matching supply to demand may also require the changing, shifting, or substitution of resources, e.g., right sizing equipment, creating multifunctional roles, dedicating resources to a single high-demand activity, substituting automation for manual tasks, and vice versa.

Goal #4: Eliminate Waste

> ⊣⊢ Lean Perfection Standard: ". . . economic combination . . . of resources at any given time."

Waste is defined as any activity or resource that destroys value or consumes resources without creating value for the patient or the Healthcare Enterprise. By its very nature waste adds unnecessary cost to any process. Lean doctrine has codified waste into eight generic forms: defects, oversupply, waiting, not fully utilizing people's abilities, transportation, inventory, motion, and excess processing.

Waste exists in both Healing Pathways and Business Pathways. Do not assume that "core" Healing Pathways add value by definition or, conversely, that "enabling" Business Pathways do not add value. The broader concept of *value creating* must be applied. For example, "enabling" business processes such as hiring, training, and retaining skilled resources, maintaining medical equipment and facilities, processing insurance claims, and conducting payment transactions are all necessary to deliver primary care, and, thus, create value.

Conversely, value-destroying wastes such as long queues of patients waiting for treatment, administering unnecessary clinical tests, and extra processing of patient information consume vital healthcare resources, constrain necessary patient services, slow patient processing, and drive up costs while reducing patient, staff, and physician satisfaction.

Goal #5: Reduce Supply Lead Time

> ⚓ Lean Perfection Standard: "Instantaneous satisfaction of a demand . . . with the optimal economic combination and sequencing of resources at any given moment in time."

By reducing supply lead time in combination with extending demand lead time (Goal #2) a Healthcare Enterprise gives itself the best opportunity to *instantaneously* satisfy customer demand *"with the optimal economic combination and sequencing of resources at any given moment in time."* Pursuing *Perfect Care* requires that Value Stream Maps, which depict supply activities, be analyzed from a total lead time perspective; that is, the total time it takes to complete a series of tasks or activities that produces a useful output.

Reducing supply lead time improves the ability to

o handle multiple demands more efficiently;

o improve planning and scheduling flexibility; and

o improve response time to unplanned events.

Lead time is the sum of the activity cycle time, batch delays, and process delays. Batch delays are periods of waiting for similar tasks to be fully completed, e.g., completing multiple patient histories before entering them into the medical records information system. Process delays are the periods of waiting between successive tasks, e.g., waiting for the physician to enter his or her formal diagnosis and treatment information into a patient's medical record before closing it out for any given event.

> ⊬ Tip: In some organizations, lead time or cycle time reduction goals drive the entire lean initiative. While this approach does drive resource efficiency, it does not ensure that supply is matched to demand (Goal #3). Thus supply lead time reduction initiatives must follow, not lead, the lean initiative. Goal #1: Define Demand, must lead. Missing the mark of matching supply to demand is the most egregious of lean wastes.

Goal #6: Reduce Total Costs

> ⊬ Lean Perfection Standard: ". . . optimal economic combination and sequencing of resources . . ."

Lean is not a cost-reduction initiative; it is an investment optimization initiative. If deployed as intended, Lean optimizes the healthcare organization's investment in services and supporting resources. Investments in underutilized or wasted resources, inefficient or ineffective processes, inadequate or incompetent human capabilities, and so on are extremely costly—at times so costly as to cause the financial demise of the Healthcare Enterprise. By applying lean value stream goals in the correct order, supported by the correct application of lean methods, a Healthcare Enterprise will expose costly value-destroying wastes while charting a path towards resource optimization that inherently matches supply to demand.

Making It Happen

Consider these thought starters when deploying lean goals.

Achieving Goal #1: Define Demand

Developing a true understanding of how much and how often patients will desire services is challenging. Demand encompasses both the Healing Pathway clinical services (the patient's BIG D) and the enabling Business Pathway operational and administrative services (the small d). Lean doctrine suggests that the patient's BIG D should act as the driver for Business Pathway operational and administrative services (the small d). Thus the BIG D and the small d must be inextricably linked.

How Do I Do It?

1. Begin your lean initiative activities by understanding patient (BIG D) or business process (small d) demands by conducting a Process-Quantity (P_cQ) analysis, in which P_c is the service being performed and Q is the forecasted or actual quantity demanded. Refer to Chapter 6, Continuous Flow, to learn how to construct a P_cQ analysis.

2. Fully describe processes so that it is clear who the customers are and what demands must be met.

3. Make logical decisions about how you group and rank the P_c of your P_cQ analysis by the nature of the services being performed.

4. Analyze patterns of demand by forecasted demand (maximum/minimum) per hour/day/week/month, actual demand, seasonal fluctuations, and evolutionary demand (demand typically associated with changes in service offerings). Review demand occurrence (frequent or sporadic) to determine if takt time is an appropriate statistic to estimate service requirements.

5. When demand varies significantly in quantity and frequency, consider the use of a six-step statistical pattern analysis (1) classify data into categories; (2) combine these categories into a set of patterns; (3) indicate selected patterns; (4) re-arrange the demand according to pattern group; (5) count the number of these demands; and (6) summarize this demand-counting in tabular form.

6. When demand is relatively frequent and thus predictable, use takt time to determine the pace at which services should be delivered. Refer to Chapter 12, Standard Operations, for how to calculate takt time.

Achieving Goal #2: Extend Demand Lead Time

Demand lead time is time that passes between the moment that a demand is known by the patient (or customer) and the time it is communicated to the healthcare provider or its representatives. Recall that the patient owns demand in the Healing Pathway. This BIG D demand varies considerably by type, the ability to detect it, and the ability to accurately diagnose it. This is often true of demand created by customers of Business Pathways, the small d. In all cases, the earlier that actual demand is detected, the sooner healthcare resources can be planned for, alerted, scheduled, and ultimately engaged. Extending demand lead time, when coupled with reducing supply lead time (Goal #5), provides the greatest possible resource flexibility in responding to customer demands of varying urgency and timing. An example of this combination occurs when Emergency Medical Technicians (EMTs) call ahead (Goal #2, Extend Demand Lead Time) to Emergency Departments (EDs) (Goal #5, Reduce Supply Lead Time), alerting them to the nature of the patient's condition.

How Do I Do It?

1. Understand the nature of demand per Goal #1.

   1a. Determine the demand drivers for Healing Pathways (the BIG D) by analyzing patient and market data.

   1b. Determine the demand drivers for Business Pathways (the small d) by capturing activity data.

2. Determine likely causes (drivers) of demand. Determine whether sufficient data exists to reliably predict their occurrence, quantity, and frequency. Use pattern and statistical analysis of these drivers to guide the Healing Pathway and the Business Pathway design decisions.

3. Establish Healing Pathway and Business Pathway practices that enable the organization to sense changes in demand. For example, monitor patient symptoms to determine if certain viruses are spreading throughout a community. Monitor

changes by insurance carriers to determine if patient admissions and/or administrative processes have to be modified.

4. Integrate forecasted and actual demand information into all planning and resource-scheduling activities.

Achieving Goal # 3: Match Supply to Demand

The BIG D demand is owned by the patient in the Healing Pathway. This is an important premise. The goal is to *match supply to demand*, not *demand to supply*. It is the customer's decision to match demand to supply, meaning they choose their healthcare provider. So, do not confuse when and how many healthcare services are to be made available with demand—these are supply decisions owned by the healthcare enterprise. Ideally, the supply of healthcare resources is only made available at the time of demand. In reality, supply resources must exist prior to the occurrence of a demand, and, by any measure, this is a substantial investment. How well supply is matched to demand often determines the winners and losers among healthcare service providers.

How Do I Do It?

1. Construct a Process Route Table (Ch. 6) based on the results of the P_CQ analysis to determine if services can be grouped by like activities.

2. Apply queuing strategies (Ch. 5) to determine the approach to sequencing and executing services that best matches supply to demand.

3. Apply continuous flow methods (Ch. 6) to design the optimal sequence of service activities, estimate

1 | The Lean Objective 21

resource requirements, and forecast supply lead time to minimize customer wait time.

4. For time- and task-intensive services, prepare a Standard Operations Combination Chart (Ch. 12) to understand the task, associated cycle times, periods of waiting, and other sources of waste.

5. Prepare a Standard Work Flow Diagram (Ch. 12) based on input from the Process Route Table to determine if activities can be physically organized to achieve improved flow.

6. Conduct a capacity analysis (Ch. 12) based on known demand drivers for service resources (human, materials, technology, equipment, and so on). Quantify resource requirements, basic demand requirements, and the nature of the service tasks.

7. Develop standard operations (Ch. 12) to guide performance of services performed in both Healing and Business Pathways.

8. Evaluate performance using the applicable metrics of effectiveness, efficiency, utilization, cycle time, and total investment (Ch. 13).

Achieving Goal #4: Eliminate Waste

Waste is defined as any activity or resource that destroys value or consumes resources without creating value for the patient or the Healthcare Enterprise. By its very nature waste adds unnecessary cost to any process. In order to see waste you must be able to imagine perfection—Perfect Care as the output of Healing Pathways and perfect execution as the output of Business Pathways. If you can, imagine the following.

- Services are only provided to fill a patient or business customer demand.

- There is immediate response to patient or business customer needs.

- There are zero service errors or product defects.

- Delivery of the product and execution of the service is instantaneous.

- There are no underutilized or overutilized resources.

- The service is delivered with the optimal combination of resources, such as people, processes, facilities, equipment, and technology, to achieve the lowest possible investment costs.

The Eight Types of Waste

✠ Hint: use the acronym **DOWNTIME** as a mnemonic for the eight wastes.

So what wastes might you see? Lean doctrine has codified waste into eight generic forms:

D Defects

O Oversupply

W Waiting

N Not fully utilized

T Transportation

I Inventory

M Motion

E Excess Processing

defects, oversupply, waiting, not fully utilizing people's abilities, transportation, inventory, motion, and excess processing.

Defects. Process outputs (throughputs) that contain errors and omissions per expectations and requirements of the patient and/or customer. Defects frequently require rework such as redrawing fluid samples or taking more x-rays. Unfortunately defects such as administering the wrong medications can also cost lives or impede patient healing.

Oversupply. Providing more services than the patient/customer needs right now or that are no longer needed. Examples include excess facilities, medical equipment, supply inventories, medical tests, and procedures.

Waiting. Patient, customer, and internal resources waiting idly on the availability of necessary resources such as people, equipment, information, and so on, at the time of need. Patients waiting in the ED to be examined or sitting idly awaiting lab results are common forms of waiting. A less visible but no less common example is a patient waiting for an appointment or scheduled procedure because of resource constraints. Waiting does not require a designated room.

Not Fully Utilizing People's Abilities. Not using people's mental, creative, and physical capabilities to their fullest to conduct or enhance the capabilities of Healing and Business Pathways. People work in combination with other resources such as technology, equipment, methods, and so on. Of these resources, improperly utilized or incapable people create the highest total costs drivers for the healthcare enterprise.

Transportation. Transporting patients and resources (people, equipment, supplies, etc.) is, by definition, waste because it necessitates additional time and resources. The objective is to eliminate or minimize less efficient and costly forms of transportation.

Inventory. Inventory is the supply of resources sitting idle awaiting demand. Inventory is both an investment and a cost. It is an investment to mitigate the risk of not having supply at the time of critical demand. It is a burdensome cost when demand never materializes. In a service environment inventories exist in all resources: people, supplies, equipment, facilities, and so on.

Motion. Movement of resources in the act of performing tasks, where the movement adds time but no value. Motion wastes are often found in poorly organized or designed workplaces as healthcare providers search for things they need, for example, searching for the mobile Electronic Medical Records (EMR) station. Less recognizable but no less wasteful are poorly designed medical equipment that requires extra movement of the patient or technician and poorly designed software applications that require complex movement between screens, for example, non-user-friendly EMR systems.

Excess Processing. Effort on the part of the patient, customer, and service provider that is perceived as redundant or having no meaningful value. One example is requiring a patient to fill out an address and insurance form for each successive visit when this information is already in the system.

How Do I Do It?

1. Before you launch a series of waste-reduction initiatives, consider constructing and evaluating an Enterprise Map (Ch. 2) that depicts both the Healing and Business Pathways. Use this big picture approach to identify lean initiative candidates.

2. Prioritize lean initiative candidates based on agreed-upon criteria, for example, Healing Pathways with the highest customer dissatisfaction or inordinate costs.

3. Initiate and coordinate team-based waste-reduction activities.

4. Construct Value Stream Maps to further detail the Healing or Business Pathway you are reviewing. (Ch. 3)

5. Review the Value Stream Map to identify the location, magnitude, and frequency of the eight types of wastes. Recall the DOWNTIME mnemonic previously discussed.

6. Establish metrics for identifying the magnitude and frequency of waste associated with this operation. (Ch. 13)

7. Begin waste elimination efforts by applying the six lean goals in the correct sequence. As waste elimination becomes more challenging, consider the use of proven Six Sigma statistical methods to structure root cause analysis and solution determination. Refer to *The Six Sigma Memory Jogger*™ II for useful insight.

---

8. Periodically review the effectiveness, efficiency, cycle time, and investment metrics to identify and eliminate waste as it occurs.

Achieving Goal #5: Reduce Supply Lead Time

Reducing supply lead time, the time needed to complete a service activity from start to finish, is one of the most effective ways to reduce waste and lower total costs. Lead time is broken down into three basic components:

1. **Cycle time.** This is the time it takes to complete the tasks required for a single work task, such as drawing a patient blood sample or completing an insurance claim form.

2. **Batch delay.** This is the wait time to complete a service task while similar service tasks are being completed or processed. An example is when patient blood samples are held until enough samples have been collected to cost effectively operate the analysis equipment. Another example is insurance claims that stack up in a virtual queue in a system database or physically sit in an administrator's inbox.

3. **Process delay.** This is the time that task outputs must wait; that is, the time between completing one task and the start of another successive task. An example of a process delay is when the patient and physician await lab results before treatment is administered. Another example is the days, if not weeks or months, it can take to get an insurance claim through all the associated process delays.

✦ Tip: The relationship between demand lead time and supply lead time is critical. The goal is to extend demand lead time while reducing supply lead time. This gives your organization the most flexibility in matching supply to demand. Both lead times have cycle time, batch delay, and process delay components.

How Do I Do It?

The steps your improvement team must take to reduce lead time are similar to the ones you take to eliminate waste.

1. Before you launch a series of supply lead time reduction initiatives, consider constructing and evaluating an Enterprise Map (Ch. 2,) that depicts both the Healing and Business Pathways. Use this big picture approach to identify lean initiative candidates.

2. Prioritize lean initiative candidates based on agreed-upon criteria; for example, Healing Pathways with the highest customer dissatisfaction or inordinate costs.

3. Initiate and coordinate team-based supply lead time reduction activities.

4. Construct Value Stream Maps to further detail the Healing or Business Pathway you are reviewing. (Ch. 3)

5. Calculate the time required for the value-added steps of the Healing or Business Pathway. This represents the best-case time for the service process as it is currently designed.

6. Review the Value Stream Map to identify where you can reduce lead time. Brainstorm ways to make the

total lead time equal to the time required for the value-added steps that you calculated in Step 5.

7. Apply queuing strategies (Ch. 5) to improve lead times.

8. Determine what constraints in resource capacity or availability exist in the process and develop a plan to either eliminate them or manage them more efficiently.

9. Apply continuous flow strategies (Ch. 6) to improve lead times.

10. Establish metrics to identify and measure service task cycle times and batch and process delays. (Ch. 13)

11. Validate effectiveness of lead time improvement initiatives through ongoing metrics.

Achieving Goal #6: Reduce Total Cost

Healthcare Enterprises must invest in Healing and Business Pathway capabilities in advance of patient demand, the BIG D. Investments in the wrong healthcare services are by definition waste. Investments in the right healthcare services are costly if they are delivered poorly and require more resources than anticipated.

Guidance on what healthcare services to provide is not the domain of lean principles or methods. However, once services are defined lean methodologies clarify the nature of demand, the requisite resources, the prescribed work methods, and their expected costs or investment requirements.

Cost-Optimization Methods

Use one or more of the methods listed on the next page to identify places to optimize the costs related to Healing and Business Pathways. These methods are also useful for analyzing and estimating resource investments during the service design process.

o **Target Costing.** This involves determining the investments required of a future or current healthcare service so that it can generate the desired contribution margins, per target pricing objectives. Target costing traditionally consists of investment factors that enable leadership to break down cost factors by healthcare demand, service type, and requisite resources.

o **Value Engineering.** This is a systematic examination of service cost factors attributed to resource type and capability. Without question, it takes a combination of resources to perform a service. But what is the right or optimal combination? For instance, is it less costly to achieve the same desired service quality with three nurses and one mobile diagnostics cart, or two nurses and two diagnostic carts? Value engineering methods guide the evaluation of alternative resources, work organization, and methods—often resulting in substantial cost reductions.

o **Target Pricing.** Target pricing is about how the customer perceives the worth of the healthcare service being offered and is typically done by evaluating comparable alternatives available in the market. Target pricing logic plays out in a Prospective Payment System (PPS) in which Medicare payment is made based on a predetermined, fixed amount, that is the target price. The payment amount for a particular service is derived based on the classification system of that service (e.g., diagnosis-related groups for inpatient hospital services). Other insurers also establish target prices by classification of services, often at variance with PPS. Regardless of the method of setting prices, the Healthcare Enterprise must determine ways to maintain a going concern. Target pricing methods help illuminate how and where costs must be controlled or reduced.

The following techniques are useful for analyzing and improving the cost of Healing and Business Pathways.

- **Kaizen (i.e., continuous improvement) Costing.** Kaizen costing empowers healthcare associates to identify costly wastes and time-consuming activities by giving them insights on cost drivers, cost of resources, and how costs are allocated to their work processes. Significant lean initiatives are often evaluated for potential cost benefit before they are undertaken, with the expectation that lean efforts will indeed result in cost savings or more efficient use of resources, that is cost avoidance.

- **Activity-Based Costing (ABC).** ABC systems allocate resource costs, first to specific service activities and then in sum to the service by customer type. For example, ABC would provide useful methods for allocating claims processing capabilities for specific Healing Pathways.

- **Cost Maintenance.** These practices monitor how well each Healing and Business Pathway adheres to cost standards set by the Healthcare Enterprise.

The adherence to standardized practices (Ch. 12) supports the cost maintenance, target costing, and kaizen-costing objectives.

How Do I Do It?

1. Total cost analysis activities should be built into all significant lean project initiatives where resource investments are anticipated.

2. Before you launch a series of total cost reduction initiatives, consider constructing and evaluating an Enterprise Map (Ch. 2) that depicts both the Healing and Business Pathways. Use this big picture approach to identify lean initiative candidates.

3. Decide whether cost reduction efforts will be applied to new or existing Healing and Business Pathways.

4. If new Healing or Business Pathways are the focus of your lean efforts, consider the use of target pricing, target costing, and value engineering methods.

5. If existing Healing or Business Pathways are the focus, consider applying ABC costing, kaizen costing, and cost maintenance to assist your investment improvement initiatives.

  ⊹ Tip: If a Healing or Business Pathway is inherently costly, first consider applying the lean enterprise techniques identified in this book. Then focus associate efforts on reducing total costs.

TWO

ENTERPRISE MAPPING

What Is an Enterprise Map?

The Enterprise Map is a high-level diagram depicting the content and relationship of core Healing Pathways and enabling Business Pathways capabilities. Once diagrammed, the Enterprise Map capabilities and resources are evaluated against the *Lean Perfection Standard*.

> ⚬ Instantaneous satisfaction of a demand, in the form, time, place, cost, and experience desired by the customer; doing so with the optimal economic combination and sequencing of resources at any given moment in time.

Core vs. Enabling Process Classification

Healing Pathways by definition are "core" processes of a Healthcare Enterprise. A *core process* is defined as a sequence of activities that produces the primary service offerings. In a healthcare setting, such processes include therapeutic (physical, occupational, respiratory, medical psychology, nursing, etc.) and diagnostic (medical laboratory, imaging, cardiology, emergency medicine, etc.) services.

Business Pathways can be both "core" and "enabling" processes. Business pathways such as registration, access, medical records, and the supply chain are considered core because they directly impact the patient. Support and other informational services such as human resources, information systems, accounting, engineering, maintenance, and indirect material supply are considered enabling processes.

Recall Goal #4: Eliminate Waste (Ch. 1): Lean traditionalists tend to look at enabling processes as waste or non-value-adding. We disagree. It is impossible to classify a successful Human Resource department that recruits, staffs, trains, and continually improves nursing skills as anything but value adding.

Why Use It?

Healthcare resources must work together to effectively diagnose and care for patients, the primary focus of core Healing Pathways, while efficiently utilizing the resources made available through enabling Business Pathways. Enterprise Mapping simplifies activities and complex relationships into an *understandable form* useful for baselining and directing performance improvement activities.

By applying color-coded ratings of effectiveness, efficiency, resource competencies, and integration of core and enabling activities, the Enterprise Map can

o select and prioritize lean initiatives;

o provide clear insights regarding Healing Pathways capabilities;

- provide clear insights regarding Business Pathways capabilities;

- reveal activities that cross multiple departments and services;

- evaluate resources such as people, information technology, equipment, standards of care, and so on according to their capabilities and impact on Healing and Business Pathways;

- make readily apparent through "color-coded" ratings capability gaps, duplications, disconnects, and misunderstandings between different functional areas;

- baseline "as-is" capabilities that can be readily compared to imagined and actual "future state" capabilities; and

- easily align actual costs and proposed investments useful for calculating the cost benefit for Healing and Business Pathways lean initiatives.

What Does It Do?

The Enterprise Map is a visual analysis tool of incredible power and adaptability. Its only limit is the imagination of those who use it. Much like the Toyota A3 process discussed in *The Lean Healthcare Implementer's Field Book*, it attempts to portray multiple levels of information on a single page. It can be crafted to show current state capabilities, imagined future state, and before-and-after comparative benchmarks—ultimately connecting all Healing and Business Pathway activities, directly or indirectly, to the bigger objective of *Perfect Care*.

─╫─

-#- Tip: Do not be tempted to delve too deeply and too quickly into Healing and Business Pathway details during enterprise mapping activities. The details will reveal themselves in Value Stream Maps, Service Blueprints, Standard Operations Combination Charts, Process Capacity Tables, Standard Workflow Diagrams, and Standard Operations Sheets.

Example: *Healing U is a Level I Trauma Center with two Ambulatory Surgery Centers. Each ASC operates an Emergency Department while providing outpatient surgery and diagnostic services.*

As a Level I Trauma Center, Healing U is required to

o have specialists in trauma surgery, orthopedic surgery, neurosurgery, surgical critical care, rehabilitation medicine, and emergency medicine to quickly and adequately provide care;

o have specialists in anesthesiology, radiology, plastic surgery, oral and maxillofacial surgery, and internal medicine readily available;

o have an operating room dedicated solely to trauma patients;

o provide community injury prevention programs;

o provide professional education for physicians, nurses, emergency medical services personnel, and physician liaisons;

o conduct resident training in general surgery, orthopedic surgery, and neurosurgery; and

o conduct research.

Figure 2-1 is a simplified version of Healing U's Enterprise Map before ratings and color-coding is applied.

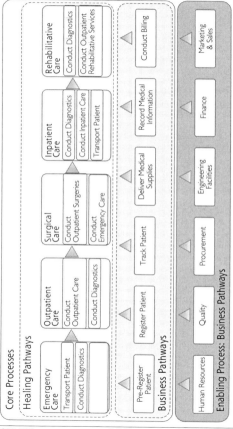

Figure 2-1—Healing U's Simplified Enterprise Map

Enterprise Map: Healing U – Level 1 Trauma Center & ASC

Core Processes

Healing Pathways

Emergency Care	Outpatient Care	Surgical Care	Inpatient Care	Rehabilitative Care
Transport Patient	Conduct Outpatient Care	Conduct Outpatient Surgeries	Conduct Diagnostics	Conduct Diagnostics
Conduct Diagnostics	Conduct Diagnostics	Conduct Emergency Care	Conduct Inpatient Care	Conduct Outpatient Rehabilitative Services
			Transport Patient	

Business Pathways

Pre-Register Patient	Register Patient	Track Patient	Deliver Medical Supplies	Record Medical Information	Conduct Billing

Enabling Process: Business Pathways

Human Resources	Quality	Procurement	Engineering Facilities	Finance	Marketing & Sales

©2012 GOAL/QPC

2 | Enterprise Mapping 37

Healing U's Core Processes consist of both Healing Pathway and Business Pathway activities. Notice the use of high-level "verb-noun" descriptors and a likely flow of activities. In the previous diagram, enabling processes are described with nouns only, reflecting a capability, not a department.

How Do I Create an Enterprise Map?

Take the following steps to create your own Enterprise Map.

Step 1: Build the Enterprise Map Template

Assemble a small team of resources who broadly understand the inner workings of your healthcare enterprise. Do not fear a lack of insight on all activities; this is a by-product of the mapping exercise itself.

Draw large "blocks" of core and enabling capabilities, as shown in Figure 2-1. This will serve as your template for adding and subtracting information as you gain insight. Notice that Healing U does not use the term Emergency Department, which is an organizational description. Emergency Care is a capability description.

- Use verb-noun descriptions for the core processes you are mapping.

- Use the highest-level descriptions; do not be tempted to go too deep too fast.

⊞ Tip: The ability to quickly revise, color-code, and disseminate the newest version of the Enterprise Map is critical, as such Enterprise Maps are typically produced and disseminated in electronic media, such as Microsoft PowerPoint, Visio, Excel or AutoCAD, with whole sections or individual functions hyper linked to more detailed diagrams, metrics, and associated documents.

3. Add activity flow arrows to your Enterprise Map. Use block arrows enabling you to color-code both arrow outlines and their fills to signify different rating criteria.

4. If external suppliers, customers, agencies, etc. play a big role in enterprise activities, be sure to include them. The SIPOC (Supplier-Input-Process-Output-Customer) diagram is an excellent way to depict external resources in your Enterprise Map. Refer to *The Six Sigma Memory Jogger*™ II for guidance on the use of the SIPOC diagram.

Step 2: Evaluate Activities

Assess the current activities against the *Lean Perfection Standard*.

⊞ Instantaneous satisfaction of a demand . . . with the optimal economic combination and sequencing of resources at any given moment in time.

○ **Effectiveness.** Does the activity produce the desired or intended result?

○ **Efficiency.** Are resources utilized productively with the minimum amount of waste?

- **Lead Time.** Is the activity being performed correctly and in the correct sequence to minimize cycle times and delays?

- **Integration.** What is the ability of the output (O) of one activity to flow uninterrupted as an input (I) to another activity? Similarly, what is the ability of information to flow uninterrupted between applications or resources?

- **Total Costs.** What is the amount invested in resources required to deliver the service offering or to perform the service process?

  ⟶ Review Lean Goals in Chapter 1 for a quick refresher on wastes, lead time, and total cost explanations.

Step 3: Apply Rating Scheme to Activities

There are multiple ways to rate activities. Be mindful that the rating scale chosen should be agreed upon by all involved if it is to be effective in motivating change. Here are a couple useful examples.

- Five-level rating scheme where the higher the score the better. Five-level ratings are excellent for discerning differences that matter without getting bogged down by analysis. This rating scheme is based on statistical evidence of performance.

5 |Blue|	*Meets expectations > 95% of the time*
4 |Green|	*Meets expectations > 90% and <94% of the time*
3 |Yellow|	*Meets expectations > 80% and <89% of the time*
2 |Orange|	*Meets expectations > 70% and <79% of the time*
1 |Red|	*Meets expectations < 70% of the time*

- Three-level rating scheme based on a combination of fact-based and anecdotal evidence. A three-level rating should be used when more levels provide little incremental information.

3 |Green| Performance trends in effectiveness, efficiency, cycle time, and total costs are improving and are considered a strength

2 |Yellow| Performance trends in effectiveness, efficiency, cycle time, and total costs are stable but are considered a target for performance improvement.

1 |Red| Performance trends in effectiveness, efficiency, cycle time, and total costs are poor or worsening and require immediate attention.

Mix and Match Rating Schemes to Improve Discernment

The Green, Yellow, Red criterion used by Healing U in Figure 2-2 may appear oversimplified, but it was deduced through analysis of factors such as patient satisfaction, physician satisfaction, total cost per patient, overtime, absenteeism, and quality and lead-time performance.

Example: *Healing U Mixed Criterion*

- Line colors reflect flow and quality of information.

- Figure fill colors reflect flow and quality of activities.

By using a mixed rating scheme, Healing U was able to assess the effectiveness of information flow for both Healing and Business Pathways.

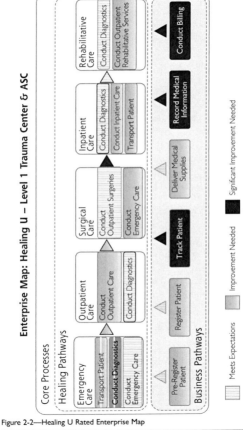

Figure 2-2—Healing U Rated Enterprise Map

As with Healing U, consider applying ratings based on multiple trends and color rating interpretations. For example, you may find effectiveness and efficiency trends going up (positive direction) and cost trends going up (negative direction). Your team may also rate the activity "green" for effectiveness (inside the block) but "red" for cycle time (the line around the block). For final analysis the team may opt to score and show the lowest color rating classification.

Example: *Healing U applies a mixed three-level rating scheme to its core processes in Figure 2-2.*

Step 4: Identify Activity Resources

Identify the specific combination of resources required to perform activities identified in the Enterprise Map. Let's review resources that are typically evaluated.

○ **People.** Also called personnel, staff, associates, contractors, human capital . . . all these terms describe people as a resource. Like all other resources, people have both abilities and a finite capacity to conduct activities. Unlike other resources, people can choose not to use their abilities to conduct a task. Mixed ratings are often applied to specific abilities, capacities, and motivations of people.

○ **Methods.** Refers to the way activities are performed: what is being done, by what resource(s), and in what sequence. Lean analysis methods focus principally on the methods that drive activities, with the ultimate goal of matching supply of healthcare services to patient demand, while optimizing resource utilization and investment.

- **Data.** Individual attributes, facts, statistics, and so on, that serve as the building blocks for information, which in turn serve as the building blocks of knowledge and insight.

- **Information Technology.** Technology deployed to capture, organize, distribute, analyze, report, and store data. It's useful to describe information technology as either software or hardware and, where necessary, to further classify these into the specific software applications or hardware technologies employed.

- **Medical Technology.** Encompasses a wide range of healthcare products that are used to diagnose, monitor, or treat diseases or medical conditions affecting humans. Medical technology may broadly include medical devices, information technology, and biotech.

- **Medical Devices.** Products used for medical purposes in patients for diagnosis, therapy, or surgery.

- **Equipment.** Apparatuses that can be generally classified by their principle use, for example, transportation, production, diagnostics, or heating and cooling. Within the context of Lean, equipment has the requirement of being maintained and/or serviced to ensure its proper performance at time of need.

- **Facilities.** Buildings, grounds, rooms, and so on that physically define, control, and protect the environment in which healthcare services are provided.

Step 5: Apply Rating Scheme to Activity Resources

It is the investment in the right resource capabilities that ultimately determines the effectiveness and efficiency of any activity. Rating resources provides clearer insight as to the sources of strengths and weaknesses of an activity. Similar to the activity level ratings, resources can be rated on effectiveness, efficiency, cycle time, integration, and total costs.

> ✦ Tip: Consider adding commentary to the Enterprise Diagram to indicate rationale for ratings. This is especially important when rating people's competencies, capacities, and motivation.

Example: *Healing U rates its Diagnostics Resources*

After reviewing its high-level Enterprise Map, Healing U focused efforts on evaluating the resources of its core emergency care activities. The "red" rating given to "Conduct Emergency Care" was principally driven by three factors. The average "Door-to-physician time" was greater than 60 minutes; the average "Door-to-inpatient bed" was greater than 7 hours; and the percentage of "Patients left without being seen (LWBS)" exceeded 5%.

Figure 2-3 shows a deep look at activity resources for conducting patient diagnostics during emergency care. The team used a mixed rating scheme, where the activity outline represented the *availability* of the resource and the fill represented the *capabilities*. Healing U felt that it needed to significantly improve both the availability and content of patient information. More effectively matching the availability of competent staffing and patient facilities to the patient condition was a tremendous challenge.

Conduct Diagnostics – Resource Assessment

Emergency Care
- Transport Patient
- **Conduct Diagnostics**
- Conduct Emergency Care

Conduct Diagnostics

Conducting diagnostics consists of ascertaining patient information through interviews, reviewing vital signs, medical histories, and analysis of specific medical testing as required or requested. Emergency care staff, facilities, and equipment must possess necessary competencies and capacities to perform patient diagnostics.

Info & Methods

- Patient Data/Info
- Diagnostic Methods
- Diagnostics Reference Database

- Patient data lacks clarity and sufficiency due to emergency conditions
- Diagnostics methods are adequate but are highly variable based on the skill levels of the ER doctors and nurses
- Diagnostics information repository is exceptional

Staffing

- Phlebotomists
- Nurses
- ER Doctors
- Technicians
- Radiologists

- ER doctor competencies vary significantly depending on medical condition
- The sporadic nature of patient conditions cause a significant challenge in assigning doctor
- There is a shortage of radiologists in the geographic area.

Facilities & Equipment

- Patient Rooms
- Diagnostic Facilities
- Diagnostic Equipment

- Lack sufficient patient rooms to enable patients to directly enter into a care environment; patients sit in the waiting room, and a significant number leave before being treated
- Past efforts to create more patient rooms have created cramped, less secure private areas, adding to the patient's anxiety levels.

Figure 2-3—Conduct Diagnostics Resource Evaluation

Step 6: Develop Future State Requirements by Using the Enterprise Map

Now is the time to begin mapping how you would like things to be done. The development of a future state Enterprise Map is a relatively straightforward process. It begins by identifying the activities that require strengthening based on current ratings and the availability of solutions (information technology, workflows and methods, decision protocols, facilities, equipment, organization structures, etc.). Once identified, the Enterprise Map provides the basis for valuing and ranking improvement initiatives.

Ultimately, the Enterprise Map drives the development of future state requirements for resources such as new information technology, work methods, required skills, and so on. In simple terms these requirements define what a resource should be able to do and the functions or tasks it should be capable of performing. Figure 2-4 is an abbreviated example of Healing U's future state requirements.

Step 7: Identify the Value Streams to be Analyzed

An inherent value of the Enterprise Map is that it enables the Healthcare Enterprise to focus limited improvement resources on the areas that will provide the greatest return on invested effort. With the addition of future state requirements as an input to value stream mapping efforts, lean initiatives are more focused, enabling those involved to envision new ways of performing vital activities.

Example: Healing U defines the Emergency Care Value Stream

Figure 2-4—Healing U Future State Requirements

Conduct Diagnostics – Future State Requirements

Emergency Care
Transport Patient
Conduct Diagnostics
Conduct Emergency Care

Conduct Diagnostics – Future State Objective

The objective is to ensure that we have the right healthcare resources available at the time of need to restore patient health as quickly and effectively as possible. This requires that the right resources correctly diagnose patient conditions at the earliest possible moment in time, that is, when the potential patient becomes aware of adverse changes in his condition.

Info & Methods

Patient Data/Info
Diagnostic Methods
Diagnostics Reference Database

Future State Requirements

• Leverage first contact resource capabilities to ascertain patient condition information prior to their arrival

• Improve use of information and telecommunication technology to enable remote consultation of doctors and specialists

Staffing

Phlebotomists
Nurses
ER Doctors
Technicians
Radiologists

Future State Requirements

• Improve recruitment and retention of radiologists

• Improve use of non-ER doctors and specialists to offset competency gaps of ER staff

Facilities & Equipment

Patient Rooms
Diagnostic Facilities
Diagnostic Equipment

Future State Requirements

• Improve the use of non-ER facility resources to reduce patient "door-to-physician time"

• Conduct analysis and redesign of ER facilities to match space utilization to likely demand, now and into the future

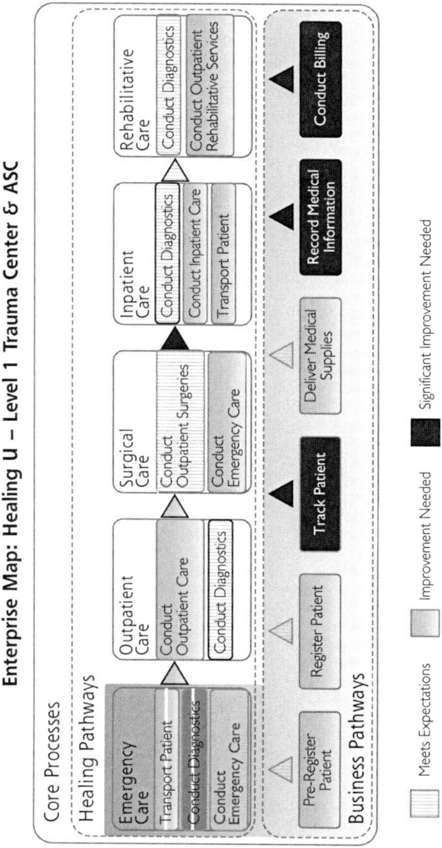

Enterprise Map: Healing U – Level 1 Trauma Center & ASC

Core Processes

Healing Pathways

Emergency Care
- Transport Patient
- Conduct Diagnostics
- Conduct Emergency Care

Outpatient Care
- Conduct Outpatient Care
- Conduct Diagnostics

Surgical Care
- Conduct Outpatient Surgeries
- Conduct Emergency Care

Inpatient Care
- Conduct Diagnostics
- Conduct Inpatient Care
- Transport Patient

Rehabilitative Care
- Conduct Diagnostics
- Conduct Outpatient Rehabilitative Services

Business Pathways

Pre-Register Patient

Register Patient

Track Patient

Deliver Medical Supplies

Record Medical Information

Conduct Billing

Legend:
- Meets Expectations
- Improvement Needed
- Significant Improvement Needed

Figure 2-5—Emergency Care Value Stream

As depicted in the previous Enterprise Map, Healing U chose to focus on the Emergency Care Healing Pathway and associated Business Pathways. Notice that Healing U does not use the term Emergency Department, which is an organizational description. Emergency Care is a capability description. Alternately, it could have assigned teams to multiple Healing Pathways. The Enterprise Map provides a graphical basis for managing multiple lean initiatives with the implicit goal of avoiding suboptimization of processes within and among departments and/or operations.

Chapter

THREE

VALUE STREAM ANALYSIS

This chapter will describe how to conduct a Value Stream Analysis. Chapters that follow will discuss how to improve value streams to optimize the flow of activities and resource utilization.

What Is a Value Stream Analysis?

The term "value stream" refers to all the process activities and associated resources necessary to deliver services to patients and the Healthcare Enterprise. A *Value Stream Analysis* maps and quantifies process activities to determine service effectiveness and resource efficiency. To ensure that lean principles are being applied, the value stream is further assessed against the lean goals defined in Chapter I and the *Lean Perfection Standard* as defined below.

> ‡ Instantaneous satisfaction of a demand in the form, time, place, cost, and experience expected by the customer; doing so with the optimal economic combination and sequencing of resources at any given moment in time.

Healing Pathways and Business Pathways Are Value Streams

We make a distinction between value streams: the **Healing Pathway** (clinical activities) and the **Business Pathway** (administrative and operational activities). This distinction helps align and focus activities on the principal objective of restoring patient health. A Value Stream Analysis is applied to either or both pathways.

What Is a Value Stream Map?

A Value Stream Map is a *uniquely defined* graphical depiction of a series of activities that work together to deliver a product or service to its intended customer. Its uniqueness is derived from the use of standardized icons and descriptions to indicate the following.

- Demand requirements

- Supply requirements

- Sequence of activities

- Flow of information

- Resource utilization (people, technology, supplies, etc.)

- Activity classification as value adding (value creating) and non-value-adding (value destroying)

- Activity data (cycle time, resource quantities, etc.)

- Activity lead times

When combined into a single diagram, both the symbols and descriptions form the basis for conducting the Value Stream Analysis.

Why Use It?

The Value Stream Map is an essential tool used to reveal waste and suboptimal resource utilization. Analysis reveals the complexities of customer demand and the gaps in resource capabilities—gaps in such areas as knowledge, resources, data, communication, coordination, integration of activities, and feedback on performance and results. Once completed, the Value Stream Analysis becomes the basis for defining and sustaining improvement initiatives.

Where to Start

Healthcare Enterprises consists of multiple value streams. The ideal starting point for choosing which value streams to analyze should be driven by an Enterprise Map assessment of capabilities. If this is not the case, we suggest working on value streams that have numerous challenges.

- Long queues or waiting periods by patients
- Excessive backlog of tasks that other work streams require as input
- Excessive rescheduling or delays in scheduled events
- Excessive multitasking that stretches resources to their limit
- Excessive overtime or absenteeism
- Significant amount of manual paperwork or double-triple rekeying of information

Example: *Healing U Emergency Care Value Stream* (EC)

Using the results of the Enterprise Map assessment, Healing U chose to conduct a value stream analysis of its Emergency Care practices (EC) (refer to Ch. 2 for decision process). Figure 3-1 shows the emergency care pathway selection on the Enterprise Map.

Step 1: Review Lean Goals

Now is the time to make sure that you have a clear vision of what you are trying to do by applying lean principles and practices to a value stream. Imagine a perfect process against these goals.

Step 2: Determine the Scope of the Value Stream Map

The SIPOC table shown in Table 3-1 is often a useful tool for scoping the Value Stream Map.

Table 3-1—Emergency Care SIPOC

Emergency Care SIPOC

Suppliers	Inputs	Process	Outputs	Customers
EMT	EMT Diagnostics	Access	Treatment	Patient
Patient	Lab Diagnostics	Sign-in	Disposition	
Patient Transport	Patient w/Ailment/ Condition	Triage	Patient w/ Restored Health	
		Registration		
		Evaluation		
		Treatment		

⌗ SIPOC is an acronym for Supplier, Input, Process, Output, and Customer. SIPOC tables are used to develop a high-level understanding of the process that is under study, including upstream and downstream links. Refer to *The Six Sigma Memory Jogger™ II* for guidance on constructing the SIPOC diagram.

Figure 3-1—Emergency Care Pathway

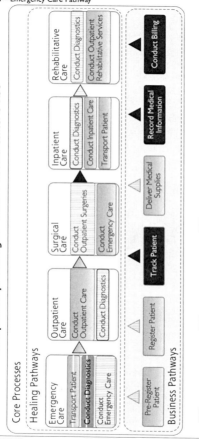

Enterprise Map: Healing U – Level 1 Trauma Center & ASC

Core Processes

Healing Pathways

Emergency Care	Outpatient Care	Surgical Care	Inpatient Care	Rehabilitative Care
Transport Patient	Conduct Outpatient Care	Conduct Outpatient Surgeries	Conduct Diagnostics	Conduct Diagnostics
Conduct Diagnostics	Conduct Diagnostics	Conduct Emergency Care	Conduct Inpatient Care	Conduct Outpatient Rehabilitative Services
Conduct Emergency Care			Transport Patient	

Business Pathways

Pre-Register Patient — Register Patient — Track Patient — Deliver Medical Supplies — Record Medical Information — Conduct Billing

▲ Meets Expectations
△ Improvement Needed
▲ Significant Improvement Needed

Step 3: Develop Value Stream Mapping Team Charter

The charter should provide the specifics of the scope of activities to be mapped. Narrow, do not broaden, the focus of your value stream mapping efforts by being very specific about the Healing or Business Pathways to be mapped.

Step 4: Assemble the Right Team

It is important that the value stream mapping team consist of resources who know the work activities, who understand the inputs and sources of supply required, who can identify all resources needed to perform tasks (e.g., software, special equipment, and supplies), and who understand the requirements or demand characteristics of the outputs being produced.

Step 5: Get to Know the Value Stream Standardized Icons

Each team member must understand the meaning and use of Value Stream icons. They are organized as follows.

o Activity Flow

o Scheduling

o Push – Pull

o Material Flow

o Data and Information Flow

o Lead and Cycle Time

o Lean Improvement

	Customer	The customer(s) of the value stream throughput.
	Activity	The top of the icon shows the name of the activity. The body indicates resources, information, or a relevant lean enterprise technique. If the activity requires a person to perform it, use the person icon inside the activity icon.
	Information Management	The hardware and software resources used to conduct activities.
	Supplier	External suppliers that provide resource to the value stream.
	Data Table	List of data that characterize the activity and metrics that describe its performance.
	Service Request	A document used to initiate the service activity.
	Material Request	A document used to obtain materials, special equipment, or tools from a designated area.

<table><tr><td>◄ June 11 ►</td></tr><tr><td>M T W T F S S</td></tr><tr><td>1 2 3 4 5</td></tr><tr><td>6 7 8 9 10 11 12</td></tr><tr><td>13 14 15 16 17 18 19</td></tr><tr><td>20 21 22 23 24 25 26</td></tr><tr><td>27 28 29 30</td></tr></table>	**Scheduled Queue**	Indicates that services will be delivered on a scheduled basis. Estimates of service duration or time standards are used to schedule service activities into available time slots.
●●●●○	**Prioritized Queue**	Shows the activities that have a backlog of work to be performed or have customers waiting for service based on a prioritization scheme.
⟶ FIFO ⟶ First In - First Out	**FIFO Queue**	Indicates that services will be delivered on a first-in, first-out (FIFO) basis

▬▬▶	**Push**	Push movement of service activity outputs. Shows the movement of activity outputs that are "pushed" by the process rather than being requested by the customer.
- - - - ▶	**Pull**	Pull movement of service activity outputs. Shows the movement of activity outputs that are requested by the customer, not "pushed" by the process.

Material (Output) Flow Icons

	Automated Movement	Indicates that automation is used to move activity outputs from one process to another.
	Ambulance	Shows the movement of patients, supplies, etc. by ambulance.
	Fire Truck	Indicates the presence of fire department engaged in the delivery of medical services.
	Truck Shipment	Shows the movement of resources by truck.
	Air Shipment	Shows the movement of resources by plane.
	Transport Arrow	Shows the direction and/or sequence of movement. Typically combined with air, truck, ambulance, etc., icons.
	Inventory	Indicates the inventory of resources such as medical supplies, pharmaceuticals, rooms, and beds.

	Storage	Shows storage area (centralized, local, etc.) where supplies, materials, special equipment, and tools are kept.
	Safety/Buffer Stock	Shows locations where extra items are kept to ensure that supplies do not run out.

> Data & Information Flow Icons

	Data Upload	Upload of data from an information technology application.
	Data Download	Download of data from an information technology application.
→	**Manual Infomation Flow**	Shows information that is transferred by hand.
⇢	**Electronic Info./Comm.**	Shows information that is transferred electronically.
information type	**Information Type**	Indicates the type of information being communicated; typically used with a communication arrow.

❯ Lead & Cycle Time Icons

	Timeline Segment	Shows the amount of value-added and non-value-added time by activity.
	Delay	Indicates how much time an activity waits in a batch or process delay. Also used to show how long a person waits in a queue.
	Time Totals	Sums all value-added and non-value-added time across the value stream.

❯ Lean Improvement Icons

	Constraint (Bottleneck)	Shows which activity(s) constrain or limit the progress of the value stream.
	Kaizen Burst (Continuous Improvement)	Shows the existence of waste or value-destroying activity.
Performance Boards	**Performance Boards**	Indicates that process objectives and results have been posted in an operation's work area.

STRETCH	**Stretch Objectives**	Shows where stretch objectives for fostering improvement have been set for specific activities or for the value stream as a whole.
Standards	**Standards**	Shows where standards of care and/or operational standards have been established for the activity.
	Visual Management	Shows that visual management techniques have been applied.
ERROR PROOF	**Error Proofing**	Shows that error proofing methods and technologies have been applied.
Quick Changeover	**Quick Changeover**	Indicates that quick changeover techniques have been applied.

Constructing the Value Stream Map

Now that you have selected the value stream and have oriented yourself to the icons, let's begin the mapping process. Follow these steps in constructing the Value Stream Map.

Step 1: Define Demand

It is essential that patient and/or customer demand is quantified before one attempts to optimize supply resources. Demand analysis typically includes

o potential demand (maximum demand);

o actual demand (historical demand);

o future demand (predicted market changes in demand); and

o evolution of demand (product/service lifecycles influence on future demand).

Supply must deliver to demand at the time of demand, in the quality and quantity demanded—but what if demand is a constantly moving target in timing, quantity, and variation of output?

Takt time is the available service time divided by the customer demand rate—in short, the frequency in which a given customer demand occurs. Given the nature of service demand, only use takt time as the broadest estimate of customer demand.

⊣⊢ Tip: Use Takt Time as a guide, not an absolute.

You can calculate takt time by using the following formula:

$$\text{takt time} = \frac{\text{available daily service time (i.e., hours of operations)}}{\text{required daily quantity of output (i.e., customer demand)}}$$

Theoretically when the value stream makes resources available more frequently than takt time, overcapacity occurs; less frequently, undercapacity occurs.

Example: *Healing U performs EC services over a 24-hour period (1440 minutes). It performs 12 Level 5 resuscitations per day. Its resuscitation takt time is 1440 minutes/12 = 120 minutes. Therefore, every two hours on average it requires medical resources to perform resuscitation activities.*

In practice, Healing U forecasts the nature and timing of demand (refer to Table 3-2) knowing that the actual demand is driven by the timing of the patient's condition. Healing U uses the process quantity (P_cQ) analysis discussed in Ch. 5, Continuous Flow, to quantify the magnitude and frequency of demand variation. Then it uses Six Sigma statistical methods to determine likely times of the day, week, month, season, or year when particular demands are more likely to occur. In combination, the P_cQ and Six Sigma analytics help quantify resource capability and availability requirements.

Example: *Healing U analyzed its EC patient demand profile.*

Table 3-2—EC Patient Demand Profile

EC Patient Demand Profile
Avg. Daily Demand – 120 pts./day
Lev. 1 Resuscitation – 12 pts./day (10%)
Lev. 2 Emergent – 36 pts./day (30%)
Lev. 3 Urgent – 36 pts./day (30%)
Lev. 4 . Semi-urgent – 24 pts./day (20%)
Lev. 5 Non-urgent – 12 pts./day (10%)

Step 2: Map Value Stream Activities

Use flowcharting techniques to map value stream activities.

- ◆ Tip: Often a process flowchart is integrated into the SIPOC diagram, indicating the sequence and integration of activities. Figure 3-2 depicts the SIPOC incorporating a process flowchart, ultimately serving as the basis for the Value Stream Map.

- ◆ The process flowchart enables the value stream analysis team to identify the actual flow or sequence of events. Refer to *The Six Sigma Memory Jogger™ II* for guidance on flowcharting methods.

Figure 3-2—SIPOC and Process
Flowchart of Emergency Care

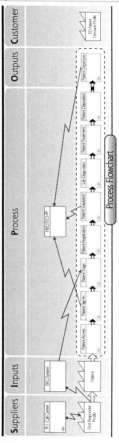

Step 3: Validate Value Stream Activities

Conduct a quick physical or virtual tour of the value stream to view the end-to-end Healing or Business Pathway activities, resources, and information flows. Consider the following as you validate value stream activities.

o Expect individual differences in perception of reality. Resolve difference to ensure the most accurate value stream map possible.

o Consider using sticky notes, which can be easily rearranged while your team comes to a consensus, or use a pencil and eraser to draw and refine your map.

o Observe the value stream in action. Interview team members from different shifts performing similar activities.

o Verify your observations against documented standards, policies, and procedures.

o Perform sequential screen captures as a way to document the flow of tasks and information within software applications.

o Record exactly what you see without making any judgments. There is no right or wrong.

Step 4: Construct the Value Stream Map by Using Standardized Icons

Consistent use of symbols will help improve communication and understanding, resulting in better analysis of one or more value streams.

Example: *Figure 3-3 is Healing U's Emergency Care Value Stream Map of the EC using the standardized icons. Take time to review the use of each symbol and associated data.*

Figure 3-3—Healing U Emergency Care Value Stream Map

See full detail on next two pages

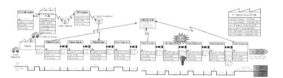

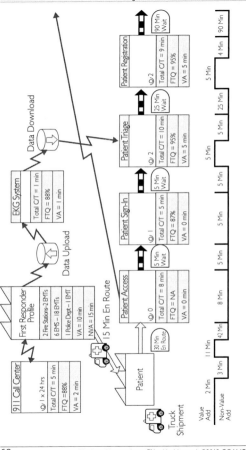

Continued on next page

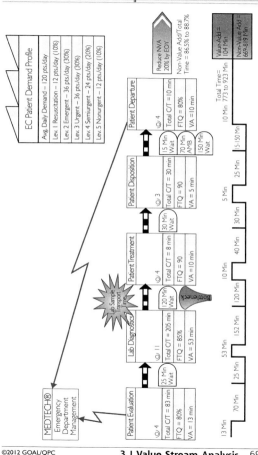

EC Patient Demand Profile

| Avg. Daily Demand – 120 pts/day |
| Lev. 1 Resuscitation – 12 pts/day (10%) |
| Lev. 2 Emergent – 36 pts/day (30%) |
| Lev. 3 Urgent – 36 pts/day (30%) |
| Lev. 4 Semiurgent – 24 pts/day (20%) |
| Lev. 5 Nonurgent – 12 pts/day (10%) |

Reduce NVA 20% by EOY

Non-Value Add/Total Time = 86.5% to 88.7%

MEDTECH®
Emergency Department Management

Patient Evaluation
Q 4
Total C/T = 83 min
FTQ = 80%
VA = 13 min
25 Min Wait

Lab Diagnostics
Q 11
Total C/T = 205 min
FTQ = 85%
VA = 53 min
Lab Sample Transport
120 Min Wait
Bottleneck

Patient Treatment
Q 4
Total C/T = 8 min
FTQ = 90
VA = 10 min
30 Min Wait

Patient Disposition
Q 3
Total C/T = 30 min
FTQ = 90
VA = 5 min
15 Min Wait

Patient Departure
Q 4
Total C/T = 10 min
FTQ = 80%
VA = 10 min
70 Min A*I*B
150 Min Wait

Total Time =
10 Min 773 to 923 Min

Value-Add = 104 Min
Non-Value Add = 669-819 Min

13 Min | 70 Min | 25 Min | 53 Min | 152 Min | 120 Min | 10 Min | 40 Min | 30 Min | 5 Min | 25 Min | 15 150 Min

©2012 GOAL/QPC

Step 5: Determine Lead Times for Value-Added and Non-Value-Added Activities

During data collection, capture cycle time of each activity, noting both batch and process delays. Make note of whether activities are performed in real time and whether they are performed in batches. Record if the activity requires multiple resources to review or approve it before proceeding to the next activity.

Step 6: Identify and Quantify Activity Queues

Identify all activities where the patients, associates, or work wait in a queue. Indicate how the queues are prioritized and sequenced.

If activities are performed in batches, show the size of the batches, how often they occur, and the average time of the *batch delay*. If the activity must go through multiple resources for review or approval, indicate average *process delays*.

Create a lead-time chart at the bottom of your Value Stream Map, showing the value-creating and value-destroying activity lead times. (Refer to Figure 3-3.)

Step 7: Pursue Value Stream Perfection

Consider the following methods contained in this book to help you perfect the value stream.

Apply Continuous Flow Methods

Use continuous flow methods to achieve the shortest possible lead times. From a customer perspective, this is always good. Ask yourself if your value stream has large backlogs of work and numerous delays. (See Ch.6)

Apply Queuing Strategies

Use queuing strategies to improve management decision making around the elimination of long patient waits, backlogs, and long batch and process delays. (See Ch. 5)

Apply Visual Management Methods

Use visual management methods to create a well-organized and well-maintained healthcare workplace that enables both customers and associates to operate in a safe and proper manner, which ensures quality results. (See Ch. 7)

Apply Error-Proofing Methods

Use error-proofing techniques to reduce errors and ensure that no defects are being passed from one activity to the next and, ultimately, to your customer. (See Ch. 8)

Apply Quick-Change Methods

Use quick-change methods to improve activity methods and sequencing, enabling efficient delivery of multiple services using similar or different resources. (See Ch. 9)

Apply Kanban Systems

Use Kanban systems to improve reordering and scheduling of the supply of materials that are frequently used. Be cautious using these systems for infrequently demanded materials. (See Ch. 10)

Apply Total Productive Maintenance (TPM) Methods

Use TPM methods to improve overall equipment effectiveness—availability, output quality, performance, and overall total ownership costs. (See Ch. 11)

Apply Standard Operations Methods

Use standard operations to further analyze, improve, schedule, document, and control value stream activities—incorporating lean methods to ensure the most efficient and effective use of resources. (See Ch. 12)

Apply Lean Metrics

Establish lean metrics for your value stream to ensure that you are meeting demand, lead-time, waste-reduction, and cost objectives. (See Ch. 13)

FOUR

SERVICE BLUEPRINTING

The customer's perspective matters, and matters most in the lean Healthcare Enterprise. When value stream activities require customer interaction to achieve the desired result, apply Service Blueprinting methods.

What Is Service Blueprinting?

A Service Blueprint is a tool for simultaneously depicting the service process, the points of customer contact, and the evidence of service *from the customer's point of view*. It was introduced by Lynn Shostack in her article, "Designing Services That Deliver," in *Harvard Business Review*, January–February 1984.

Elements of the Service Blueprint

The Service Blueprint consists of the alignment of three main blueprint elements: *Onstage, Lines of Interaction and Visibility*, and *Backstage*.

Onstage consists of four components: *Evidence, Customer Actions, Emotional Icons*, and *Onstage Contact Actions*. *Lines of Interaction and Visibility* are demarcations indicating various interactions and what the customer can or cannot observe. *Backstage* consists of *Backstage Contact Actions* and *Support Processes*.

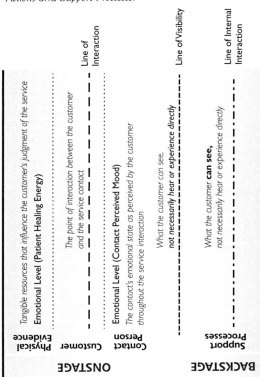

Figure 4-1—Service Blueprint Elements

Onstage

Evidence

Evidence is defined as the noticeable resources or actions to which the customers are exposed that can influence their judgment of the service.

Customer Actions

Customer actions are steps in the process that the customer performs. For example, the customer recognizes that he or she has a medical need and makes contact with a healthcare provider.

Emotional Icons

Emotional icons are symbols that indicate the emotional state of the customer during interactions. In the Healing Pathway these icons can be used to represent relative levels of *"healing energy."* See Figure 4-2 for example emotional icons.

Figure 4-2—Emotional Icons

Onstage Contact Actions

Onstage contact actions are performed in the presence of the customer. For example, the EMT arrives at the patient's location and begins the diagnostic process.

Lines of Interaction and Visibility

Line of Interaction

The line of interaction is a graphical depiction of where customers and/or internal resources interact with each other.

Line of Visibility

The line of visibility is a graphical depiction of where customers can observe service activities.

Backstage

Backstage Contact Actions

Backstage contact actions are performed outside the customer's view. For example, the EMT unloads diagnostic gear from the ambulance prior to directly reaching the patient.

Support Processes

Support processes include any actions taken by other members of the service team that support the activities of the service providers. For example, the ED nurse receives patient information transmitted by the EMT and begins preparation for patient arrival.

Service Blueprints vs. Value Stream Maps

The Service Blueprint focuses on the *interaction* between the customer and various onstage, backstage, and support service providers. It also describes the "mood" or "atmosphere" in which the service is delivered. Thus the Service Blueprint is the essential design of the service concept or intent. In contrast, the Value Stream Map depicts service delivery with emphasis on activity sequence, timing, and resource utilization, with the goal of optimizing service delivery and efficiency. Both tools are necessary for truly understanding and designing lean processes.

Preparing a Service Blueprint

Where to Start

At this juncture in your lean transformation efforts you may have already narrowed your efforts to select value streams. If you have chosen Healing Pathways or Business Pathways where customer interaction is an essential activity, the Service Blueprint unquestionably applies.

Example: *Healing U focuses on the activities of its EC Value Stream Map—Identification of patient need to the ED physician's evaluation. Refer to the following Figure 4-3.*

Figure 4-3—Healing U's EC Value Stream Map: Identification of Patient Need to Physician's Evaluation

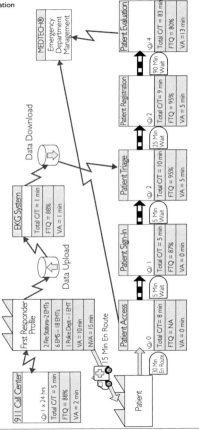

Be the Customer

Don't imagine the customer—be the customer. Produce a real-life documentary, entitled "*A Day in the Life of Me!*" Achieve customer empathy by walking in their shoes.

Map the Primary Interactions

The appropriate level of detail is based on the customer's direct experience and on the primary contact and support actions.

Use the Customer's Words

Describe the interaction using terms that the customer would use. For example, the Healing U Service Blueprint depicted in Figure 4-4 has the patient "giving symptoms" four times; each contact person may describe the interaction with the patient differently based on the purpose of his or her questioning.

Record Physical Evidence

Equipment, facilities, supplies, and so on with which the customer must interact or which is a necessary tangible resource that the customer perceives as integral to the service delivery.

Depict the Customer's Emotions

The objective is to record the most frequently occurring customer emotions at various points in the service delivery. Indicate whether the customer's emotional response to the contact improves, worsens, or has no impact on the contact's ability to complete his or her service tasks. In the case of Healing Pathway Service Blueprints, indicate if the patient's healing energy is impacted.

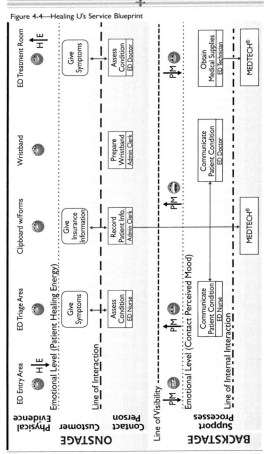

Figure 4-4—Healing U's Service Blueprint

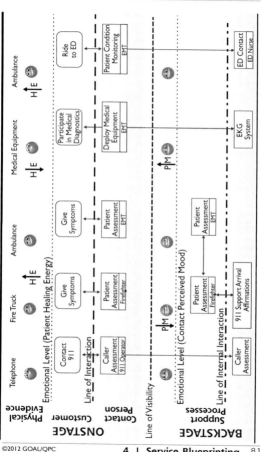

Depict the Perceived Contact Mood Level

Similar interactions may elicit different emotional responses between the customer and the service contact. When blueprinting the emotional levels, it is the customer's perception that matters. Use the same emotional scale, perhaps color-coded differently, to map the contact's mood as perceived by the customer.

Identify Backstage Line-of-Sight Support Processes

Identify processes, resources, and/or factors that may impact satisfaction with the services that exist in the line of sight of the customer. Examples include visual displays, orderliness, cleanliness, odors, sounds, conversations, other customer interactions, and so on.

Identify Backstage Line of Internal Interactions Support Processes

Identify processes, resources, and/or factors that may impact satisfaction with the services that exist internal to the contact's organization. These factors are not within the line of sight of the customer. Examples include information systems, supervision, interaction with support personnel, and so on.

Analysis of the Service Blueprint

Lean goals apply to the Service Blueprint, just as they do to the Value Stream Map. A unique goal of the Service Blueprint is making the intangible tangible—namely the customer's experience with service delivery. Focus on improving the service experience in total.

Look for the Eight Impediments to Healing

If a Healing Pathway is a focus of your service, look for the Eight Impediments to Healing. These are the equivalent of wastes in a value stream and should be eliminated to the greatest degree possible. The eight impediments to healing can be remembered using the mnemonic SICKNESS.

The Eight Impediments to Healing

Stress & Anxiety	A common state of patients created by the malady that brought them to the hospital; uncertainty and fear about what might be wrong with them and unfamiliarity with the hospital setting.
Inactivity & Waiting	Idle and unproductive time created when staff cannot tend to patients at a rate appropriate to their treatment.
Coldness or Apathy	An aloofness or distancing from the patient by one of his or her caregivers.
Knowledge Gap	The lack of information patients have about what is wrong with them, what is happening to them, and what is going to happen and when.
Neglect	The absence of steady interaction and information sharing with the patient.
Embarrassment	A negative patient experience caused by a lack of dignity in the treatment process.
Submission & Helplessness	A state of learned helplessness exacerbated by information, power, and social status differentials.
Statistic	Depersonalization of patients: "the chest pain in Room 13," "five boarders," etc.

Just as eliminating waste from value streams stimulates flow and throughput, eliminating impediments from Healing Pathways stimulates patient recovery. The tasks associated with a Healing Pathway analysis are therefore twofold: eliminate barriers to process flow and eliminate impediments to patient healing.

Incorporate the Eight Enablers to overcome service impediments to the greatest degree possible. These apply to all Healing Pathways and Business Pathways that require interaction with the customer.

The Eight Impediments and the Eight Enablers

Stress & Anxiety	**C**alm & Comfort	Be composed and exude confidence in your health care capabilities.
Inactivity & Waiting	**P**rogress	Interact with the patient/customer in a way that keeps him or her moving through the service process. (Refer to Ch. 5, Continuous Flow, and Ch. 6, Queuing Strategies, for more insight.)
Coldness or Apathy	**C**aring & Warmth	Adopt the attitude that all customers/patients are valued and deserve your best attention.
Knowledge Gap	**A**bundant Communication & Understanding	Inform and enlighten, do not lecture and/or judge any lack of insight.
Neglect	**E**ngagement	Acknowledge the customer/patient's existence; stay connected throughout the service delivery.
Embarrassment	**D**ignity	Do not purposefully cause a customer/ patient to "lose face." Adopt the attitude that all humans have value and should be treated as such.
Submission & Helplessness	**R**espect & Empowerment	Engage the customer/patient as a real and useful contributor to service delivery.
Statistic	**S**pecial	People have feelings, numbers don't. You provide services to people, not numbers. Your service exists because of them, and this is indeed special.

Chapter FIVE

DEMAND QUEUING STRATEGIES

We know of no healthcare system that can afford to make all the necessary resources available around the clock, waiting for patients to show up at its doors. Yet the very essence of a lean healthcare system is matching supply to demand exactly, where patient demand can occur at any time in virtually any place.

What Are Demand Queuing Strategies?

Demand queuing strategies help healthcare providers prioritize and sequence customer demand in all of its various forms.

For example, Healing U knows that the nature of demand for emergency care can vary according to severity of demand. Using a five-level triage scale such as *Resuscitation, Emergent, Urgent, Semiurgent, and Nonurgent* is an example of a demand queuing strategy.

Demand can also vary by the time of day (cardiac arrests), the season of the year (allergies, flu), the occurrence of events (sports-related injuries), and so on. Whereas a significant portion of patient demand can be both sporadic and infrequent, the follow-up visits can be planned and scheduled well in advance.

What Do They Do?

Demand queuing strategies are based on the premise that not all demands are equal, thus not all supply responses need to be equal. Demand queuing strategies help sort and ultimately manage these inequalities, so when demand is clearly critical, supply is there at the time of need, and when demand is routine, supply responds fairly from the customer's perspective.

The Four "Queue" States

As customers seek your services, they may find your healthcare system in one of four "queue" states.

---

1. **Unmet Demand.** Patients can't find a healthcare provider to meet their needs at the time of the need. This is known as a latent or unmet demand queue. This queue may be the result of the unique nature of the patient demand or the lack of available healthcare services within a service area.

2. **Demand Exceeding Optimum Capacity.** A healthcare provider exists; however, patients must wait until capacity becomes available. Demand queuing strategies are often driven by the availability of one or more constrained resources such as the doctor, the nurse, or the CT scanner. Such constraints are often cited as the reason for inordinate waiting times or patients leaving without being seen.

3. **Matched Demand and Supply.** Customer service requirements are met with the optimal combination of resources at the time of need. Steady-state or highly predictable demand increases the probability of matching supply to demand, whereas highly variable demand, both in quantity and frequency, increases the challenge.

4. **Excess Capacity.** Idle resources add undue cost to both the Healing and Business Pathways. As a reminder, resources are people, equipment, technology, facilities, and so on. It takes a combination of resources to perform value stream activities, any or all of which can be classified as excess.

Understanding Demand

It is incomprehensible that organizations undertake initiatives to match supply to demand with little to no insight into demand. Lacking this insight, many organizations adopt the "supply seeking demand" mode of operation, where they define the services they provide, they establish hours of operations, and they make resources available against a schedule, all while competing against organizations that apply similar tactics. This may be necessary for the conduct of business, but can mask the true nature of customer demand.

So what do you do? Simply put, conduct ongoing and frequent analysis of customer demand. Consider these four demand parameters when conducting your analysis.

o **Forecasted Demand.** Forecasting demand is typically driven by arbitrary estimates or statistical analysis. In either case, forecasting demand requires different analytical approaches when demand is frequent and consistent than when it is infrequent and sporadic. This book will not delve into forecasting methods.

o **Actual Demand.** Actual demand is based on the number of times a customer demands a service from your organization, not the number of times a demand is met. For example, demand for EC services would include those who received treatment, those who left without being seen, and those who were diverted en route due to resource constraints. The same logic must be applied to schedule healthcare services.

○ **Demand Pattern Fluctuations.** Quantifying seasonality, time of day, and activity-driven demand patterns is useful for matching supply to demand; for example, the cold and flu season, heart attacks occurring principally in the morning or in the early evening, and increases in broken bones during football season.

○ **Evolutionary Demand.** As your healthcare organization changes its services, so the associated demand also changes. Be mindful of the tendency to overestimate demand to justify investment in new services.

Example: Healing U undertakes a statistical study of customer demand by triage classification for its EC services. The study was based on a Process (P_c)–Quantity (Q) Analysis. Figure 5-1 is a snapshot of its Process–Quantity (P_cQ) Analysis. The P_cQ Analysis ranks processes by quantity of their execution. In Healing U's case, processes were defined by unique customer demands requiring a service response. Insight on how often a demand occurs by the nature of the service response is critical to creating a lean healthcare system.

Figure 5-1—Healing U – EC Triage P_cQ Analysis

Triage Class	(P_c)rocess Medical Condition	Rank	(Q)ty. Avg. Day	Cumm. Total	% of Total	Cumm. %
U	Moderate Pain	1	16	16	13	13
E	Acute Chest Pain	2	12	28	10	23
U	Broken Bones	2	12	40	10	33
SU	Abdominal Pain	2	12	52	10	43
E	Overdose (if unconscious)	5	8	60	7	50
U	Burns	5	8	68	7	57
SU	Earache	7	6	74	5	62
SU	Upper Respiratory Symptoms	7	6	80	5	67
R	Cardiac Arrest	9	5	85	4	71
E	Multiple Injuries	9	5	90	4	75
E	Congestive Heart Failure	9	5	95	4	79
NU	Minor Sprains	12	4	99	3	83
E	Severe Allergic Reaction	13	3	102	3	85
R	Unconsciousness	14	2	104	2	87
NU	Flu	14	2	106	2	88
NU	Minor Cuts	14	2	108	2	90
NU	Medication Refills	14	2	110	2	92
R	Respiratory Failure	15	1	111	1	93
R	Active Seizure	15	1	112	1	93
R	Anaphylactic Shock	15	1	113	1	94
R	Insulin Shock	15	1	114	1	95
R	Septic Shock	15	1	115	1	96
E	Serious Infection	15	1	116	1	97
E	Hyperthermia	15	1	117	1	98
E	Hypothermia	15	1	118	1	98
NU	Cold	15	1	119	1	99
NU	Dental Pain	15	1	120	1	100
	Total		120			

Frequency and pattern analysis, as shown in Figure 5-2, provides additional insight. For example, cardiac arrests tended to occur in the A.M., while acute chest pains and congestive heart failures more likely occurred in the P.M. Saturdays appear to be the day that the ED would most likely see broken bones and multiple-injury patients.

Figure 5-2—Healing U – EC Triage Frequency and Pattern Analysis

Triage Class	Medical Conditions	Avg. Day	Cumm. Total	%	Cumm. %	AM/PM	Total	Mon	Tues	Wed	Thu	Fri	Sat	Sun	AM/PM
U	Moderate Pain	16	16	13	13	AM	8	3	–	–	–	–	–	–	AM
						PM	8	–	–	–	–	–	2	2	PM
E	Acute Chest Pain	12	28	10	23	AM	0	–	–	–	–	–	–	–	AM
						PM	12	3	–	–	–	–	3	2	PM
U	Broken Bones	12	40	10	33	AM	2	–	–	–	–	2	–	–	AM
						PM	10	–	2	–	–	–	–	4	PM
SU	Abdominal Pain	12	52	10	43	AM	10	4	–	–	–	2	4	–	AM
						PM	2	–	–	–	–	–	–	–	PM
E	Overdose (if unconscious)	8	60	7	50	AM	3	1	–	–	–	–	–	–	AM
						PM	5	–	–	–	–	2	2	2	PM
U	Burns	8	68	7	57	AM	7	–	–	–	–	2	3	2	AM
						PM	1	1	–	–	–	–	–	–	PM
SU	Earache	6	74	5	62	AM	6	2	2	–	–	–	2	–	AM
						PM	0	–	–	–	–	–	–	–	PM
SU	Upper Respiratory Symptoms	6	80	5	67	AM	6	2	2	–	–	–	–	2	AM
						PM	0	–	–	–	–	–	–	–	PM
R	Cardiac Arrest	5	85	4	71	AM	5	2	–	–	–	–	2	–	AM
						PM	5	–	–	–	–	–	–	–	PM
E	Multiple Injuries	5	90	4	75	AM	5	–	–	–	–	2	3	–	AM
						PM		–	–	–	–	–	–	–	PM
E	Congestive Heart Failure	5	95	4	79	AM	4	–	–	–	–	–	–	–	AM
						PM								15	PM
						Total		22	11	6	6	13	22		**Total**

Selecting the Right Queue

Recall that the goal of a lean healthcare system is to match supply to demand at the time required by the demand. Given that patient and customer demand occurs according to its parameters, not yours, the highest priority demand may find itself: 1) arriving at the back of the queue; 2) waiting in the queue; or 3) being served at the front of the queue. This queuing strategy must decide at any time, if the customer or work queue needs to be reshuffled or if resources need be added or subtracted to match supply to demand. So how do you decide which queue is right for the healthcare service being offered? Here are some factors to consider.

Customer Impact

- When does the true demand occur? Note that this is not the same as hours of operation.
- Does the urgency of customer demand vary significantly, requiring a prioritization system?
- What is the impact of waiting on the customer?
- Does increased patient flow mean increased sales?

Business Impact

- Does the queue design require more or less investment in resources than an alternative?
- What impact does the customer waiting have on the healthcare provider?
- Can we gain a competitive advantage by providing services that are closer to demand, based on customer priorities, and more efficient and effective than those of our competitors?

Workflow Impact

- Does the queue selected enable you to achieve continuous flow? (Ch. 5)
- Does the queue selected promote the elimination of "lean waste"?

Queue Designs

As you answer the questions regarding customer, business, and workflow impact, consider the following four basic queuing designs.

1. **First In, First Out (FIFO) Queue.** FIFO is designed to support "equal priority" demand as it occurs and in the order in which the healthcare provider is prepared to respond. It requires the healthcare provider to clearly define its services, define its hours of operation, and make the requisite resources available.

2. **Scheduled Queue.** A scheduled queue attempts to allocate time slots based on estimated lead times of the healthcare activities. Schedule slots can be fully allocated based on "equal priority" FIFO demand or partially allocated to allow for higher-priority demand as it occurs. Scheduled queues require knowledge of resource availabilities and time required to perform standardized services. The ability to schedule services aides in managing customer timing expectations while optimizing resource utilization.

3. **Prioritized Queue.** A prioritized queue gives varying levels of importance, and therefore position in the queue, based on the nature of the demand.

Typically, priority is based on the impact on the customer—both positive and negative. The five-level triage example we have used in previous chapters is a prioritized queue. Priorities may also be based on compliance, certification, and/or legal requirements imposed by the government or the healthcare industry.

4. **Combination Queue.** It is common for service providers to combine FIFO, Scheduled, and Prioritized queue designs to maximize resource utilization while enhancing the customer's sense of control (refer to the Psychology of Waiting section of this chapter). Rarely does one queue design fit all healthcare customers' demand patterns.

Consider the Psychology of Waiting When Designing Queues

Perhaps the most frustrating result of a mismatch between supply and demand is that customers are often waiting in what appears to be an interminable queue. By definition, waiting is a lean waste. However, in practical terms even in the best lean systems someone or something is waiting. Here are some well-researched tips for handling customers who must wait in a queue of any type ("Losing 'Waits'" in The TMTC Journal of Management, Dr. Mukta Kampllikar, citing the work of Edgar Osuna).

o Unoccupied time feels longer than occupied time.

o Preprocess waits feels much lengthier than in-process waits.

o Anxiety makes a wait feels longer.

- Uncertain waits are longer than explained waits.
- Unfair waits are longer than equitable waits.
- The more valuable a service, the longer the time that people are willing to wait.
- Solo waits feel longer than group waits.

There are two principle strategies for addressing wait times. The first is to effectively manage customer expectations of when healthcare services are available. This does not mean that because they know your hours of operation or that they are scheduled to be seen that they are satisfied with either. Therefore, the second strategy is to improve service capacity by making the right resources available at the right time and by executing both Healing and Business Pathway activities in the most efficient manner possible. This is the lean way.

From Queuing Theory to Practice—The Emergency Severity Index (ESI)

Recall that the patient owns demand, the BIG D of the Healing Pathway. The Emergency Severity Index (ESI) represents a practical example of demand queuing theory in action. How does ESI queue the BIG D? See the ESI Triage Algorithm from ESI Triage Research Team, LLC out of Concord, MA. The ESI approach defines demand and matches supply to demand. This is lean thinking at work.

Next Steps in the Lean Transformation

Building on the Value Stream Map (Ch. 3), the insight gained from Service Blueprinting (Ch. 4), and a thorough understanding of the types and nature of customer demands, now is the time to begin designing an optimal future state value stream that truly matches supply to demand.

Chapter SIX

CONTINUOUS FLOW

Imagine streams of activities, each one flowing into another, effortlessly, without interruptions, with a constant movement as if drawn by a greater purpose—*Perfect Care*. Imagine these streams widening or narrowing, rising or lowering, accelerating or slowing, depending on the urgency of the customer or patient need. Imagine continuous flow on a mission.

What Is Continuous Flow?

Continuous flow is the sequencing, aligning, balancing, and pacing of activities and resources into an uninterrupted stream. For example, Patient #1 enters the ED, Patient #1 signs in, Patient #2 enters the ED, Patient #1 moves to triage, Patient #2 signs in, Patient #3 enters the ED . . . Patient #49 enters the ED, Patient #1 departs ED . . . and so the flow goes.

When to Use It

Let's quickly trace a lean analysis journey.

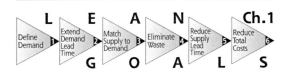

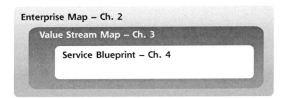

Figure 6-1—Lean Transformation Analysis Roadmap

Figure 6-1 gives an overview of the lean analysis roadmap we have traversed thus far. We began by discussing goals that drive the lean transformation in Chapter 1. We mapped the enterprise to access capabilities at the highest levels in Chapter 2. In Chapter 3 we focused on specific value streams that would yield the capability improvements we desired by our enterprise mapping activities. In Chapter 4, we constructed and analyzed Service Blueprints, where value streams relied on patients and customers to engage in the service delivery. In Chapter 5 we took a deeper look at the nature of customer demand and associated queuing strategies, which will ultimately drive the design of the Healing and Business Pathways.

Now is the time in our lean transformation to apply continuous flow methods that move us toward matching supply to demand (Goal #3), eliminating wastes (Goal #4), and reducing supply lead time (Goal #5) while remaining steadfast in our pursuit of the *Lean Perfection Standard*.

- ‑#‑ Instantaneous satisfaction of a demand in the form, time, place, cost, and experience expected by the customer; doing so with the optimal economic combination and sequencing of resources at any given moment in time.

Why Use It?

Applying continuous flow methods to Healing and Business Pathways allows us to reduce *activity cycle times* and, where practical, eliminate process delays and batch delays, thus reducing supply lead time. Continuous flow activities are designed to maximize our ability to meet multiple and ongoing customer demands with the optimal combination of resources at a pace that ensures quality of work and patient safety while avoiding long queues and overburdened and idle resources.

Time Measurements that Matter

Customer Takt Time

$$\text{takt time} = \frac{\text{available daily service time (i.e., hours of operations)}}{\text{required daily quantity of output (i.e., customer demand)}}$$

Demand Lead Time

- o Demand Lead Time = moment in time when the service provider becomes aware of the need; moment in time when the customer/patient suspects and/or acts on a service need

Supply Lead Time

- o Supply Lead Time = Cycle Time + Batch Delays + Process Delays

  Where:

  - o Cycle Time = time required to complete a singular task
  - o Batch Delay = total time to complete a batch of similar tasks (one cycle time)
  - o Process Delay = total time between the completion of last task (singularly or in a batch) and the beginning of the next sequential task

When applying the continuous flow methods, attempt to *maximize demand lead time* and *minimize supply lead time*, thus providing the *greatest flexibility* of matching supply resources to the *customer's takt time*.

Achieving Continuous Flow

Figure 6-2—Continuous Flow Pathway

Output
Continuous Flow Value Stream

Standardize Operations	Validate & Improve Flow	Identify Inhibitors – Enablers	Develop Flow Concepts	Determine Flow Suitability	Evaluate Current State
Standard Operating Procedures	Continuous Flow Plan	Future State Value Stream Map	Process-Oriented Layouts	Service Groupings	Process Quantity Analysis (PQ)
Continuous Flow Analytics	Flow Validation	Lean Solutions	Virtual "Information" Flows	Demand Drivers	Process Route Table
Resource Capability Analytics	Lean Documents	Multifunction Right-Sized Resources	Lead Time Estimates	Service Characteristics (Must Haves)	Standard Workflow Diagram
Demand Analytics	Continuous Flow Environment	Multiskilled Workforce	Balance Activities	Service Characteristics (Nice to Haves)	Standard Operations Combination Chart (SOCC)

Input
Current State Value Stream Map

The *Continuous Flow Pathway* shown in Figure 6-2 was designed to assist you in stepping through the often challenging process of streamlining operations. The *Continuous Flow Pathway* phases include

- Input – Output;
- Evaluate Current Conditions;
- Determine Flow Suitability;
- Develop Flow Concepts;
- Identify Flow Inhibitors/Enablers;
- Validate and Improve Flow; and
- Standardize Operations.

Input – Output

You will use your current state value stream as your input; the goal is to produce a continuous flow value stream.

Evaluate Current Conditions

Evaluate Current State	Process Quantity Analysis (P_cQ)	Process Route Table	Standard Workflow Diagram	Standard Operations Combination Chart (SOCC)

The goal is to accurately characterize both the demand and supply characteristics of the value stream. Apply these tools to your current-state Value Stream Map:

P_cQ *Analysis.* The P_c stands for Process (Activity) type; the Q stands for Quantity of output, as shown in Figure

6-3 (which is excerpted from Figure 5-1). This tool helps employees understand the types of Healing and Business Pathway services provided. Analysis reveals if pathways (value streams) must deliver a narrow or wide variety of services.

Triage Class	(P_c)rocess Medical Condition	Rank	(Q)ty. Avg. Day	Cumm. Total	% of Total	Cumm. %
U	Moderate Pain	1	16	16	17	17
E	Acute Chest Pain	2	12	28	13	29
U	Broken Bones	2	12	40	13	42
SU	Abdominal Pain	2	12	52	13	55
E	Overdose (if unconscious)	5	8	60	8	63
U	Burns	5	8	68	8	72
SU	Earache	7	6	74	6	78
SU	Upper Respiratory Symptoms	7	6	80	6	84
R	Cardiac Arrest	9	5	85	5	89
E	Multiple Injuries	9	5	90	5	95
E	Congestive Heart Failure	9	5	95	5	100
	Total		95			

Figure 6-3—Healing U's P_cQ Analysis (Excerpted)

Combined with demand analyses that reveal the quantity and frequency of services, you can begin to identify which services are most suitable for continuous flow. Just know that not all processes are suitable for continuous flow. The Process Route Table provides more insight.

Process Route Table. This method depicts multiple activities within a given service area. Figure 6-4 is a sample Process Route Table developed by Healing U's EC services for its top 95% service (demand) types.

Figure 6-4—Healing U – EC Process Route Table (Excerpted)

Figure 6-4—Healing U – EC Process Route Table (Excerpted)

Patient Demand Type	Patient Triage (R, E, U, SU, NU)	Patient Registration	Patient Evaluation							
			Obtain History	Perform Focused Assessment	Obtain Vital Signs	Obtain Weight	Remove Clothing	Perform EKG	Activate Cath Lab	Administer Oxygen
Moderate Pain	⇧	●	●	●	●		○			
Acute Chest Pain	⇧	●	●	●	●			●	◑	●
Broken Bones	⇧	●	●	●	●		◑			●
Abdominal Pain	⇨	●	○	●	●		◑			
Overdose (if unconscious)	⇨	●	●	●	●	●	○			●
Burns	⇨	●	●	●	●		●			◑
Earache	⇨	●	●	●	●					◑
Upper Respiratory Symptoms	➡	●	○	●	●	●	●			●
Cardiac Arrest	⇨	●	◑	●	●	●	●	●		●
Multiple Injuries	⇨	●	●	●	●	●	●			●
Congestive Heart Failure	⇨	●	●	●	●		●	●		●

Legend

Triage	Resuscitate	Emergent	Urgent	Semiurgent	Nonurgent
	➡	●	⇧	⇨	○
Likelihood	>75%	75%<>25%		25%<>1%	
	●	◑		○	

Patient Evaluation

Insert IV	Obtain Blood Work	Remove Clothing	Conduct X-Ray	Assess Pain	Perform Comfort Measures	Insert Foley Catheter	Insert Nasogastric Tube	Immunize	Give Medication	Administer Activated Charcoal	Insert Cardiac Catheter

Preparing a Process Route Table

1. Use the P_cQ Analysis processes (P) by rank (Q) as the starting point. (Refer to Figure 6-3.)

2. Use the Value Stream Map to identify the major activities. (Refer to Figure 3-3 in Ch. 3.)

3. Where necessary break out significant tasks by activity. For example, Healing U further detailed Patient Evaluation, Lab Diagnostics, and Patient Treatment activities.

4. Place markers in each box where a specific process requires the conduct of certain activities/tasks. Healing U used *Harvey Ball symbols* ○ ◑ ● to indicate the probability that a certain activity would be executed given the variation in the patient's condition.

5. Connect the markers to show the sequence of activities. Healing U's example shows all activities occurring in a general sequence from left to right. You may decide to use sequence numbers or lines that route back and forth to show actual sequence.

Standard Workflow Diagram. The Standard Workflow Diagram is used to capture the work sequence in a physical layout. It also enables you to track the physical distances that people and materials move in order to complete a task. Refer to Chapter 12, Standard Operations, for information on how to construct a Standard Workflow Diagram. A "spaghetti diagram" is a popular method for capturing current state workflows. (See Figure 6–5.)

Figure 6-5—Healing U's ED Spaghetti Diagram

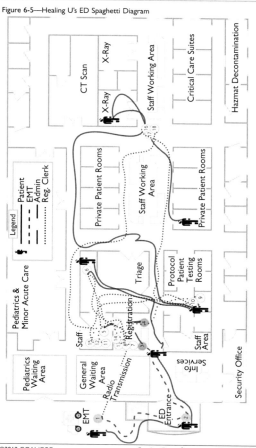

Spaghetti Diagram. The spaghetti diagram is useful for revealing opportunities to improve the physical flow of activities in your value stream. It's a straightforward way to record the path of activities by using a measuring wheel or tape measure to document distances. Rarely do actual activity paths flow in a straight line, thus the name cooked spaghetti.

Healing U's seemingly organized ED layout has both the patient and the registration clerk wandering about in what appears to be a maze.

Standard Operation Combination Chart (SOCC). Now it's time to dig into the details of each process. The SOCC provides insight into whether a given process can be "balanced" to achieve customer demand per a given takt time. Balancing a continuous flow operation requires that activities be "leveled," meaning that no process activities are waiting on another and no activity is being performed ahead of its need.

Constructing the SOCC, as shown in Figure 6-6, involves observing tasks, recording their sequence, and capturing time by the nature of the task—manual, automated, walk, and wait. Refer to Ch. 12 for preparation instructions.

Standard Operations Combination Chart (SOCC)

Process Name: Registration	Location: Emergency Department	Avg. Demand per Day: 30	Cycle: 60 Min	Takt Time: 70 Min	Gap: 10 Min	Date: August 8th	Dept: ED	Prepared by:

STEP	Operation Description	Resources	TIME (min) Manual (a)	Auto (C)	Walk (b)	Wait (d)	5	10	15	20	25
1	EMS Advanced Communication	EMT	-	30	-	-					
2	Enter ED	EMT	0.5	-	-	-					
3	Patient Access	Admin	8	-	-	-					
4	Patient Sign-in	Admin	5	-	-	-					
5	Patient Triage	Admin	5	-	-	2					
6	Take Prelim. Info	Reg. Clerk	0.5	-	-	-					
7	Walk to Registration	Reg. Clerk	-	-	0.5	-					
8	Patient Search	Reg. Clerk	0.5	0.5	-	-					
9	Walk back to ED	Reg. Clerk	-	-	0.5	-					
10	Verify Information	Reg. Clerk	0.5	-	-	-					
11	Walk back to Registration	Reg. Clerk	-	-	0.5	-					
12	Copy Insurance Card	Reg. Clerk	0.5	0.5	-	-					
13	Input Data	Reg. Clerk	0.5	0.5	-	-					
14	Print Out Labels	Reg. Clerk	-	0.5	-	0.5					
15	Build Chart	Reg. Clerk	1	0.5	-	-					
16	Walk back to ED	Reg. Clerk	-	-	0.5	-					
17	Put on Arm Band	Reg. Clerk	0.5	-	-	-					
18	Sign Consent Form	Reg. Clerk	0.5	-	-	-					
			23	2.5	2	2.5					

Manual: ......
Auto: ~~~~~
Walk:
Wait:

Determine Flow Suitability

| Determine Flow Suitability | Service Groupings | Demand Drivers | Service Characteristics (Must Haves) | Service Characteristics (Nice to Haves) |

Can your value streams be designed to achieve continuous flow? Answering this question is a function of multiple factors.

Service Groupings. Analyze the Process Route Table for potential groupings by process (demand) type. As shown in Figure 6-7, Healing U created three groups for its EC services. Group 1, for example, cardiac care demand with unconscious overdosed patients.

Continued on next page ➡

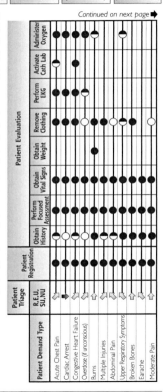

Figure 6-7—Healing U's Grouped EC Services

Continued from previous page

Legend										
Triage	Resuscitate	⬇	Emergent	⬂	Urgent	⇨	Semiurgent	⬀	Nonurgent	⇧
Likelihood	>75%	●	75%<>25%	◐	25%<>1%	○				

Lab Diagnostics				Patient Treatment								Patient Disposition					Patient Departure
Insert IV	Obtain Blood Work	Obtain Lab Samples	Conduct X-Ray	Assess Pain	Perform Comfort Measures	Insert Foley Catheter	Insert Nasogastric Tube	Immunize	Give Medication	Administer Activated Charcoal	Insert Cardiac Catheter	Prepare Release	Prepare Admissions Order	Hold Patient in ED	Admit Patient	Assign Bed	Obtain Vital Signs
●	●	●	●	●	●				●		○	◐	◐	◐	◐	◐	●
●	●	●	●						●		●	○	●	◐	●	●	●
●	●	●	●	●	●				●			○	●	◐	●	●	●
●	●	●							◐	◐		○	●	◐	●	●	●
◐	●		◐	●	●	○	○	○	●			◐	◐	◐	◐	◐	●
◐	◐		◐		●				●			◐	◐	◐	◐	◐	●
○	◐	◐		●	●				◐			◐	○	○	○	○	●
			◐		◐				●			●					
			●	●	●				●			●					
					◐				●			●					
○				●	●				●			●					●

To determine if a potential service grouping can be "balanced" use the SOCC.

Demand Drivers. When reviewing the service groupings, answer the question, *Can we make resources available in the right capacity to match service delivery to the exact nature and frequency of customer/patient demand?* Analyze the Demand Queuing Strategies (see Ch. 5) to the need for continuous flow based upon urgency of customer demand. For example, Healing U might suggest that all cardiac arrests with a triage level of Resuscitation must be processed without any delays in activity flow; whereas a patient with an earache would not.

Figure 6-8—Healing U's Cardiac Care Frequency Chart

Use the demand pattern and frequency analysis to look for likely times when certain resources are needed. As depicted in Figure 6-8,

Triage Class	Medical Conditions	Avg./Day	Cumm. Total	%	Cumm. %	AM/PM	Total	Mon	Tues	Wed	Thu	Fri	Sat	Sun
E	Acute Chest Pain	12	28	10	23	AM	0							
						PM	12	3				1	3	2
E	Congestive Heart Failure	5	95	4	79	AM	1					1	1	
						PM	4						1	
R	Broken Bones	5	85	4	71	AM	4	2	2				2	
						PM	5							4
					Total			6	2		2	1	6	4

Healing U determined that it needed to make more resources available for cardiac care in the early evening for acute chest pain and congestive heart failure. It also experiences spikes in demand for cardiac care on Mondays and Saturdays. .

Service Characteristics (Must Haves). Achieving Continuous flow requires

o activities that can be sequenced in a natural flow;

o activities whose resources (competencies and capacities) can be effectively scaled to match variations in the quantity of customer demand; and

o information systems that enable multiple value-stream applications to communicate and share data instantaneously, thus eliminating information batch delays.

Service Characteristics (Nice to Haves). Continuous flow works best when

o multifunction resources, like information technology, facilities, and equipment, can be used to conduct multiple required tasks, thus minimizing delays between tasks;

o a multiskilled workforce has the capability to perform various tasks required to ensure continuous flow;

o activities can be broken down into smaller tasks and reallocated/shared across multiple resources; and

o activities require little to no setup time or preparation time at the time of customer demand.

Develop Flow Concepts

Develop Flow Concepts	Process Oriented Layouts	Virtual "Information" Flows	Lead-Time Estimates	Balance Activities

Process Oriented Layout. Continuous flow often works best when you can minimize movement and conveyance by lining up activities according to the improved process sequence. To baseline your current activity flow, consider the use of a Spaghetti Diagram as described previously and depicted in Figure 6-5.

Figuratively, take the roof off your work area and imagine straight lines and L-shaped and U-shaped layouts for the pathways that resources must follow within and between areas. Consider the following when imagining physical workflows.

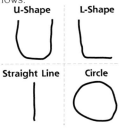

o Typically U- and L-shaped layouts are better than straight lines when attempting to maximize workforce utilization. Why? Straight lines make personnel walk farther when going back to the start of the process. In U- and L-shaped layouts, multifunctional workers can handle the first and last process activities, which are now in close proximity.

o Straight lines work if there is no requirement for a resource to travel excessively, that is from the beginning to the end of the "line."

- Avoid the enclosed circle layout design that creates processing islands where movement interferences are likely to occur between resources. Circles can be effective for certain administrative tasks where the "swivel" of a chair acts as the center point.

- In all cases, attempt to shorten the physical distance between activities.

- Be mindful of distances and transportation factors created by activities being performed on multiple floors.

Virtual Information Flow. Consider these recommendations when applying continuous flow principles to information technology.

- Leverage information technology to eliminate the need for resources to move.

- Manage information technology so that it is available at the exact time of need—now and into the future.

- Avoid gathering data that has no real value or is too little too late.

- Eliminate information bottlenecks that prevent the effective completion of value stream activities.

Lead-Times Estimates. Develop a future-state SOCC, as shown in Figure 6-6, to capture changes in tasks, sequencing, and physical and virtual information flows. The SOCC produces a more realistic estimate of lead times, including activity cycle times and batch and process delays. For details on constructing an SOCC, see Ch. 12.

Balance Activities. Use the SOCC to break down activities into smaller tasks (manual and automated) and determine if the tasks can be rearranged or broken apart to achieve a "balanced time" in cases where any one resource in the value stream is waiting or sitting idly.

Identify Flow Inhibitors/Enablers

Identify Inhibitors/ Enablers	Future State Value Stream Map	Lean Solutions	Multifunction Right-Sized Resources	Multiskilled Workforce

Identify known and predicted roadblocks to achieving continuous flow and their associated solutions.

Future State Value Stream Map. Develop a Future State Value Stream Map, paying particular attention to

o how activities flow against the priority or urgency of customer demand (see Ch. 5);

o the differences in activity cycle times that cause un-balanced flow—causing an "accordion" effect;

o flow of materials and supplies into activities—leaving either the activity waiting or leaving resources idle;

o flow of information into activities—identify where lack of information hinders activity completion;

o job definitions that minimize activity disruptions—pay attention to role boundaries that inhibit flow, especially for constrained resources; and

o resource capacity resulting in idle resources, excessive backlog, or wait time—where lacking, develop the necessary demand and supply insight to successfully match supply to demand.

Lean Solutions. Identify all potential value stream waste and apply lean methods to eliminate it.

- The eight types of waste (DOWNTIME): Defects, Oversupply, Waiting, Not Fully Utilizing People's Abilities, Transportation, Inventory, Motion, and Excess Processing.

- Methods to identify and eliminate these wastes: Value Stream Mapping (Ch. 3), Service Blueprinting (Ch. 4), Visual Management (Ch. 7), Error Proofing (Ch. 8), Quick Changeover (Ch. 9), Standard Operations (Ch. 12), and Lean Metrics (Ch. 13).

Multifunction, Right-Sized Resources. Consider how resources such as equipment, special tools, and information technology should be designed and deployed to best support continuous flow objectives. For instance:

- Does the resource need to perform multiple functions to leverage one available resource?

- Should the resource perform a single function to improve work flow and reduce lead time?

- Can the resource be easily integrated with upstream and downstream activities to perform the level of effort required at the desired pace?

Multiskilled Workforce. Similar to multifunction and right-sized resources, workforce capabilities and responsibilities are likely to change to support continuous flow designs. If this is the case, seek input from Human Resources before roles and responsibilities are changed.

Validate and Improve Flow

Validate & Improve Flow	Continuous Flow Plan	Flow Validation	Lean Documents	Continuous Flow Environment

Plan to do, do the plan.

Continuous Flow Plan. Before your lean team begins its continuous flow transformation, it should develop an implementation plan. Consider the following major plan elements.

○ Preparing the organization for change

○ Conducting trial runs and validating activities

○ Physically preparing the new work environment

○ Preparing workforce for new roles and responsibilities

○ Managing rehearsals and a "go live" event

○ Establishing standard operating procedures

○ Monitoring and improving performance

Flow Validation. Validate new operations before you go live with patients and customers alike. To avoid disruption to services, use a pilot area where you can test options and ideas. Consider involving patients and customers to engage new processes and provide meaningful feedback and insight on changes that matter most to them.

Lean Documents. Update your lean documents to reflect the chronology and the logic for your changes. Use these documents as check sheets to validate changes.

Continuous Flow Environment. Leverage written and visual cues that remind personnel and customers alike of what they are expected to be aware of and what to do. Consider the following.

- Apply visual management techniques to make the flow visually apparent while building intelligence into the service environment. (Refer to Ch. 7)

- Apply error-proofing techniques such as job aids, checklists, and visual aids, to ensure that activities are performed without error and to minimize defects. (Refer to Ch. 8)

- Create communication mechanisms for identifying and evaluating changes to continuous flow activities.

- Reset the work environment when it is least disruptive to customers and patients.

Standardize Operations

Standardize Operations	Standard Operating Procedures	Resource Capability Analytics	Continuous Flow Analytics	Demand Analytics

Establish the new work standards and protocols for operating and continually improving the new continuous flow process.

Standard Operating Procedures (SOPs). An excellent lean tool for capturing both work sequence and physical layouts is the Standard Operations Sheet (SOS) shown in Figure 6-9. It combines the best work sequence from a Standard Operations Combination Chart and the best physical workflow captured in a Standard Workflow Diagram (SWD). (Refer to Ch. 12)

You should begin drafting new SOPs during the validation phase. Be sure everyone involved knows that the SOPs are DRAFT only. Now it's time to finalize SOPs that support the new workflow.

Resource Capability Analytics. As you implement the new value stream flow, focus on the resource capabilities—which resources (people, methods, technologies, and so on)—are up to the task, and which ones need strengthening? Be prepared for confusion as both customers and employees experience the new workflow. Providing a mechanism for "How are we doing?" for customers and "How are you doing?" for employees is an essential step in a successful one-piece flow transformation.

Continuous Flow Analytics. Monitor and improve flow. The goal is to reduce overall lead time by eliminating batch and process delays and also to further reduce activity cycle time by improving how tasks are performed and/or the combination of resources that is used.

Demand Analytics. While in pursuit of *Perfect Care*, never take your eyes off your fundamental purpose: restoring patient health in the most effective and efficient manner possible. As patient and customer demand changes, so must supply. The goal is to be a patient-centered healthcare system.

Figure 6-9—Standard
Operations Sheet
(SOS)

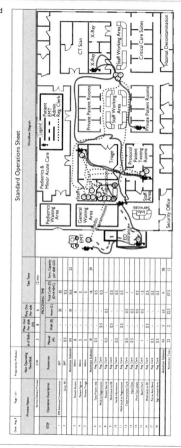

SEVEN

VISUAL MANAGEMENT

The world is devoid of all senses except for one—sight. Does sufficient intelligence exist in the environment to enable flawless execution of healthcare services?

The impact of visual management is best seen and felt when the situation demands it. When the urgency to do things right the first time is paramount—when wasted effort searching for things and figuring out what to do next must be eliminated—everyone, including the patient, must work together to ensure success.

What Is Visual Management?

Visual management is a set of techniques that

o make your service standards, such as procedures, protocols, and standards of care easily understood and visible to all required associates;

o make supplies of all types readily discernible;

o improve workplace efficiency through both physical and visual organization;

o make routes that customers and healthcare resources must traverse clear and easy to follow; and

o visually expose waste so it can be eliminated while preventing recurrence.

The essence of visual management is designing and building "intelligence" into the work environment so that resources can perform efficiently and without error.

What Does It Do?

Using visual management techniques enables your company to do the following.

1. Improve the quality of healthcare services by creating a work environment that

o alerts resources about possible errors and defects before they occur;

o detects the errors and defects that do occur and enables rapid response and correction; and

o makes visible standards for zero errors, defects, and waste.

2. Improve workplace safety and employee health by

o exposing hazards so that they can be expeditiously addressed;

o improving communication by sharing information openly throughout the company; and o creating compliance with all work standards, reporting deviations, and responding quickly to problems.

3. Improve the overall efficiency while meeting customer expectations by

o removing clutter and sources of distraction from the physical workplace (tangible objects, manuals, equipment, facilities, etc.) and virtual workplace (electronic/digital information);

o organizing both the physical and virtual workplace so that they enhance the flow of activities; and

o using visual cues, physical constraints (barriers), and other techniques to ensure that activities are performed correctly.

Why Use It?

The goal is to create an organized, uncluttered, efficient, clean, and visually appealing workplace (physical and virtual) that aids in the delivery of healthcare services.

The 5S Methodology

5S is a structure methodology to achieve visual management objectives. The 5S methodology originated in Japan, and has been adopted across industries worldwide to achieve visual management objectives. The 5S method is often conducted as a specific improvement (Kaizen) event of a *Lean Transformation*. The 5S method is summarized in Table 7-1.

Table 7-1—The 5S Methodology

5S	Japanese Term	English Equivalent	Activity
Sort	Seiri	Tidiness	Eliminate unnecessary items from the workplace.
Set in Order	Seiton	Orderliness	Apply efficient and effective storage and organizational methods.
Shine	Seiso	Cleanliness	Thoroughly clean the work area.
Standardize	Seiketsu	Standardization	Standardize improved practices in the work area.
Sustain	Shitsuke	Discipline	Commit to the new standards while constantly seeking improvement.

Preparing for a 5S Event

Before you undertake a 5S event, make sure you do the following.

o Elect a "visual management champion" to lead the program for multiple 5S events. This person's primary role is to advance 5S methods and remove any barriers that teams may encounter along the way.

o Train all involved employees about the visual management techniques and develop the plan of attack together.

- Communicate, communicate, communicate to other employees and other work areas that might be affected by the 5S event.

- Coordinate the 5S team effort with potential support resources such as maintenance, facilities management, and so on.

- Designate and prepare a "red tag" storage area for holding unnecessary materials, files, equipment, tools, and so on, that you remove from work area.

- Identify, obtain, and organize 5S supplies such as tags, cleaning materials, paint, labels, marking tape, and sign materials for use by the team.

- Make sure that all employees understand and follow health and safety procedures as changes are made.

Conducting the 5S Event

The 5S method discussion that follows has been applied to the physical workspace (facilities, equipment, materials, hardcopy files, etc.) and the virtual workplace (soft copy files, information technology, etc.). Let's begin.

1. Sort *(Seiri)*

Begin the 5S event by sorting through all of the items in your work area—emphasis on all. Your goal is to keep what is needed based on likelihood and frequency of usage and to remove everything else. Follow these steps to keep your efforts on track.

Table 7-2—Sorting Criteria

No.	Frequency of Use	Urgency of Demand
1	Never (unneeded)	Noncritical to current workplace
2	> 1 Year	Critical
3	> 1 Year	Noncritical
4	Monthly	Critical/Noncritical
5	Weekly	Critical/Noncritical
6	Daily or More	Critical/Noncritical

Thought Starters & Actions

- Give it to a work area that can use it.
- Resell as part of an investment recovery environment.
- Dispose of it without harm to the environment.

- Keep in a secure location, either with other critical items of similar nature or near the source of use.
  - Store in a centralized storage area used by multiple work areas.
  - Store with items typically used together or as part of a kit.
- Keep a record of the item in an inventory system that identifies both where used and where stored.

- For supply items determine if amount exceeds one years' worth of consumption. If so, dispose of excess according to Criteria 1.
- Store items in a less-trafficked storage area.
- Keep a record of the item in an inventory system that identifies both where used and where stored.

- Keep in a secure location, either with other critical items of similar nature or near the source of use.
  - Perhaps store in a *local storage area* used by a specific work area or adjacent work areas.
  - Store with items typically used together or as part of a kit.
- Keep a record of the item in an inventory system that identifies both where used and where stored.

- Keep in a secure and readily accessible location for the general work area.

- Keep in a secure and readily accessible location for the individual or shared workstation.

Sorting the Physical Workspace

1. Apply the sorting criteria contained in Table 7-2. Modify criteria as required to fit the nature of items to be sorted.

2. Create a running inventory of items that are likely to be kept but moved to another storage area.

3. Validate, as best you can, the actual usage of items. If disagreements on what to keep occur, try to resolve the conflict; consider who uses the item, how often is it used, and work performance impact. Beware the hoarder.

4. Attach red tags (refer to Figure 7-1) to all the items you removed from your work area and place in a "red tag" area by agreed-upon sorting criteria.

5. For items likely to be disposed, maintain in a "local" red-tag storage area for a minimum of five days. Do not allow uncontrolled removal of items from this area. Beware the hoarder.

6. After five days, move any item that you haven't needed to a "central" red-tag storage area for another 30 days.

7. After 30 days, follow your company policy for disposal of items. Track the disposal of all red-tag items.

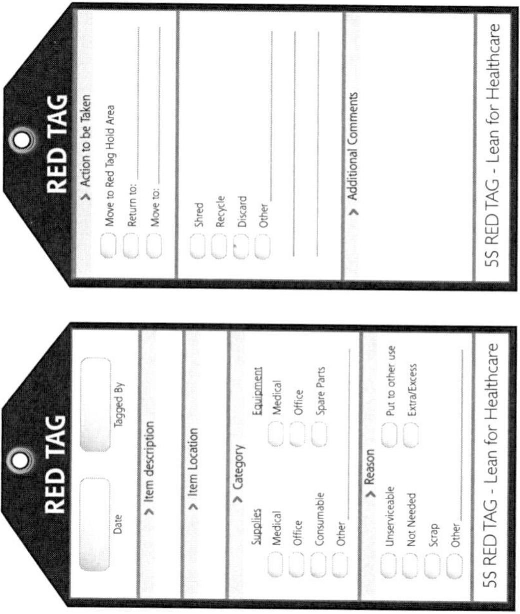

RED TAG

> Action to be Taken

☐ Move to Red Tag Hold Area
☐ Return to: _____
☐ Move to: _____

☐ Shred
☐ Recycle
☐ Discard
☐ Other

> Additional Comments _____

5S RED TAG - Lean for Healthcare

RED TAG

Date _____   Tagged By _____

> Item description

> Item Location

> Category

Supplies
☐ Medical
☐ Office
☐ Consumable
☐ Other

Equipment
☐ Medical
☐ Office
☐ Spare Parts

> Reason

☐ Unserviceable
☐ Not Needed
☐ Scrap
☐ Other

☐ Put to other use
☐ Extra/Excess

5S RED TAG - Lean for Healthcare

Figure 7-1—5S Red Tag

Sorting the Virtual Workspace

1. Apply 5S steps to organizing the virtual work on computers, file servers, application servers, and so on.

2. With the mobile computing world becoming more prevalent, many workers are using their laptops for both personal and professional

purposes. Be sensitive to both the legal and personal productivity impact when addressing this situation during the Sort process.

3. Use software discovery tools available for identifying all hardware, software applications, and associated files currently loaded in network assets. Other technology enables one to discover duplicate files, unused files, remnants of old programs, and so on. These tools are excellent for a virtual Sort process.

4. Identify what applications, virtual (softcopies) files, records, multimedia, and so on are relevant for use today or into the future.

5. The red tag area for the virtual world might be a designated space on a server, a backup drive, or a third-party service.

2. Set in Order (Seiton)

The objective of the Set in Order phase of the 5S process is to create effective storage and organizational methods that enhance the efficiency of the work activities. So let's begin.

Set the Physical Workspace in Order

1. Create a map of your workspace that shows where all the workstations, equipment, and supplies are currently located. Similar to a Spaghetti Diagram (Figure 6-5) draw lines on the map to show the steps taken by personnel in performing work tasks, including reaching for items.

2. Use the map to identify cluttered areas, wasted motion, congestion, inaccessible area, excessive distances traveled, unnecessary movement, and improper equipment and supplies.

3. Draw a map of a more efficient workspace, showing the rearrangement of every item that needs to be moved.

4. Consider the following "control points" when constructing your new layouts.

○ **Flow Alignment.** Attempt to organize physical resources and materials to support the flow of activities as identified in the Value Stream Map.

  ○ **Mobile equipment.** Identify all mobile equipment and clearly mark where it should be located when not in use. Consider using equipment-tracking software and technology to improve locating capabilities.

○ **Infrastructure Changes.** Identify potential major changes such as removal/addition of walls, repositioning of equipment, or reorganization of whole department areas as a desired future state.

  ○ Immobile equipment, structures, etc. It is sometimes impractical or impossible to move something. When this is the case conduct a P_cQ analysis (Figure 5-1) to determine and rank the type and frequency of usage.

○ **Work Instructions and Protocols.** Make work instructions and protocols both visible and readily accessible.

o **Electronic Information.** Consider placing affixed or tethered electronic and computer devices in places of most likely use, which are consistent with workflow. Where practical, consider the use of mobile devices such as tablet computers that enable information systems such as Electronic Medical Records (EMR) to be accessible anywhere at any time.

o **Stocking Levels.** Consider the impact of restocking intervals and physical space when resetting your workspace. Refer to Ch. 10 for more insight.

o **Health, Safety, and Environmental Factors.** Layouts should contribute to maintaining a safe, healthy, and environmentally compliant workplace.

o **Resource and Location Markings.** Consider using clear markings to identify people, equipment, supplies, and storage locations.

o **Customer Line of Sight.** Validate the flow of activities and placement of resources relative to the customer experience through the use of a Service Blueprint, as defined in Ch. 4.

5. Apply the "three actuals" as you analyze and improve workplace layouts. The three actuals require the 5S team to go to the actual place and talk to the actual people about the actual process.

6. Post new workplace layout in an area where it can be reviewed and commented upon by multiple resources across multiple shifts. Gather, analyze, and respond to all inputs to achieve support for changes.

7. Create the 5S relocation plan. Refer to the Set in Order Worksheet.

8. Estimate new storage by quantity, size, and weight of items.

9. Identify likely storage locations that best fit the flow of work activities and use by one or more work areas.

10. Reset work area.

Example: *Healing U established a 5S "Triage" team that reviewed the following as part of their activities.*

○ EC Value Stream Map—Figure 3-3

○ EC Service Blueprint—Figure 4-4

○ EC Triage P_cQ Analysis—Figure 5-1

○ EC Triage Frequency and Pattern—Figure 5-2

○ EC Process Route Table—Figure 6-4

○ EC Spaghetti Diagram—Figure 6-5

The 5S team determined that resource movement and locations between registration, staff area, triage, and the protocol rooms could be improved to achieve lean objectives.

Examples of changes made include the following.

○ Additional dedicated ED workstation terminal and multipurpose printer/scanner in the triage area, eliminating excess movement and waiting time by the registration clerk: Steps 7–15. (See Figure 7-2.)

Figure 7-2—Spaghetti Diagram Before and After

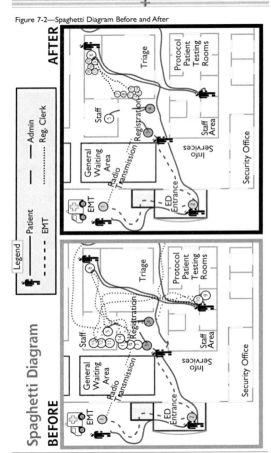

Spaghetti Diagram

BEFORE

AFTER

Legend

— Patient
— Admin
····· EMT
····· Reg. Clerk

o Integrated mobile application to record triage status and produce a color-coded wristband. (See Figure 7-3.)

Figure 7-3—Triage Tracking and
Wristband Application

o Differentiated scrub colors to make it easier for the ambulance drivers, EMTs, and patients to quickly see the differences in roles. (See Figure 7-4.)

Figure 7-4—Color-Coded Scrubs

o Organization of the triage medical supplies into kits on a trolley, thus reducing both travel and search time by triage nurse. (See Figure 7-5.)

Figure 7-5—Kitted Items in Trolley

Before changes were made, the 5S team used a Set in Order Worksheet, as shown in Figure 7-6.

Figure 7-6—Set in Order Worksheet

Set in Order Worksheet

Item to Relocate	Old Location	Proposed Locations	Approved by	Assigned to	Relocation Timing	Status
New Terminal	Reception Desk	Triage Room	DJM	SHJ	May 6	Complete
New Multipurpose Printer/Scanner	Staff Room	Triage Room	DJM	SHJ	May 6	On Order
Triage Medical Kits	Individual Items in Cabinet	Kitted Item in Trolley	DJM	EWM	May 6–7	Complete
New Triage Wristband Application	New	Mobile App	DJM	SHJ	May 15	Being Piloted

Set the Virtual Workspace in Order

1. Use the P_cQ diagram to identify and rank the type of virtual information in the work areas involved.

2. Use the Enterprise Map Ch. 2 to quickly determine scope and interconnectivity of the information flow.

3. Determine the specific information management requirements (who, what, when, why, and how) as required by the value stream activities.

4. Use the Set in Order Worksheet (see Figure 7-6) to achieve agreement on the disposition of virtual information.

5. Consider using document control and file sharing systems that define and ultimately control the placement, retrieval, updating, and purging of work-related files.

6. Apply compression and archiving methods for infrequently used or required retention documents.

7. Set up your file structures, security levels, access rights, and permissions as required.

3. Shine *(Seiso)*

Throughout the 5S activities your team has de-cluttered all forms of unnecessary items and visual distractions from targeted work areas. Consider these steps during your Shine activities.

---

1. Define "clean" requirements by work area—operating rooms, waiting areas, etc.

2. Identify and use approved cleaning tools and fluids—do not create harm from well-intentioned actions.

3. Take "before" pictures.

4. Clean/inspect equipment, storage areas, facilities, etc.

5. Report any abnormal wear or conditions that might lead to equipment failure.

6. Determine the root cause of sources of contamination and accelerated deterioration.

7. Identify ways to eliminate all sources of contamination, clutter, and other sources of distractions and to keep your workplace clean at all times.

8. Take "after" pictures.

9. Communicate results.

4. Standardize *(Seiketsu)*

Once your new work environment has been sorted, set in order, and polished, it's time to document, communicate, and, if need be, educate on new or updated:

○ storage areas;

○ locations of critical supplies and equipment;

○ locations of infrequently used supplies and equipment;

○ supply retention and disposal practices; and

○ policies, procedures, and standards.

Once you have standardized your methods (refer to Chapter 12, Standard Operations), make your standards known to everyone so that anything out of place or not in compliance with your procedure will be immediately noticed. Figure 7-7 is an example of an excerpted daily hospital room checklist.

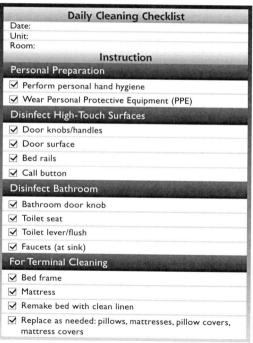

Figure 7-7—Hospital Room Cleaning Checklist (Excerpted)

5. Sustain *(Shitsuke)*

This is the hardest and perhaps the most important step of the 5S process. Old habits die hard. Psychologists suggest that we reach for habits mindlessly, setting our brains on autopilot and relaxing into the unconscious comfort of familiar routine.

The secret is not to focus on old habits, but rather to consciously guide our thoughts and actions based on new ones. This is the goal of the Sustain step: consciously focusing on the new way we have organized our workspace. As you begin the process of forming new work habits, have all involved write down their ideas for preventing the reemergence of unnecessary items, remembering to put things away, or cleaning up after the fact. Find ways to keep new procedures and work rules in the forefront of everyone's thoughts and actions.

Sustaining New 5S Habits

- Identify the habit (behavior) you would like to change or create. Be very specific. "I want to maintain a neat and orderly workspace" is not specific enough. "I will create a file and a location for that file for every document I desire to retain" is more specific.

- Describe the positive benefits of the changed habit, such as, "I will be able to find what I need at a moment's notice!" Keep reminders of these benefits nearby.

Figure 7-8—Healing U's Sustain Score Sheet

5S Sustain Score Sheet

Location: Triage Room Date: Jun 6 Auditor: DMD

Score	NA	0	1	2	3	4	5	Description of Area	Comments
Sort									
1					3			No unused/unnecessary items are located in the area	
2						4		Excess supplies are identified for dispositioning	Old battery carts stacked up in Staff area
3					3			Excess equipment has been identified for dispositioning	
Set in Order									
4							5	Medical supplies are orderly and in the designated areas	Exceptional organization
5						4		Nonmedical items are orderly and in the designated areas	
6						4		Movable equipment is in its designated area	Mobile cart left in hallway
Shine									
7					3			Work surfaces free of dust and stains	Coffee stains and foodstuff highly visible
8							5	Floors are clean in all work areas	Exceptional
9							5	Restrooms are clean	
Standardize									
10							5	Bulletin boards are organized and uncluttered	
11				2				Standards and Protocols are visible and readily available	Unable to locate "Overdose" protocol
12						4		Locations are marked and color-coded to standards	Need to mark cart storage area by cart #
Subtotal	0	0	0	2	9	16	20	Total of 47 Out of 60	78%

o Conversely, describe the negative consequences of not adopting the new habit, such as, "customers will have to wait as I search for information, leading to customer dissatisfaction." Keep reminders of these consequences nearby.

o Commit to your new habit for a minimum of 21 days. Research tells us that it takes a minimum of three weeks to develop a new habit.

o The 5S Blog. Why not? Consider establishing a blog that will enable quick feedback about new work organization and visual management techniques. The blog feed reinforces new habits and proposes new visual work processes while driving continuous improvement.

Example: *To help Sustain its 5S results, Healing U developed a Sustain Score Sheet, shown in Figure 7-8.*

Chapter EIGHT

ERROR PROOFING

What Is Error Proofing?

Error proofing is a structured method for identifying and preventing mistakes before they turn into defects. The terms error and mistake are synonymous.

What Does It Do?

Error-proofing methods enable you to discover the causes of mistakes and apply an appropriate error-proofing technique or device, ultimately preventing the occurrence of a defect. The focus of error proofing is not identifying and counting defects, for example, medical services activities gone awry. Rather, the goal is to eliminate their cause: one or more errors that occur somewhere in the process. The distinction between an *error* and a *defect* is as follows.

o An error is any deviation from a specified service process activity or task characteristic. Mistakes made in the process activities cause defects.

---

o A defect is a specific activity output that does not conform to specifications or a customer's expectations. Defects are caused by errors.

Why Use It?

Simply put, defects in the medical industry have potential life and death consequences. Thus, identifying and preventing errors that result in defects is a mandatory objective. Here are some thought-provoking statistics.

o How many U.S. patients die annually due to preventable errors?

  o 44,000 and 98,000 – Institute of Medicine (IOM) 1999[1]

  o 195,000 – HealthGrades 2004[2]

  o 99,000 due to hospital-acquired infections (HAI) – AHRQ 2008[3]

  o 7,000 due to medication errors – Kaiser Family Foundation[4]

o How many patients are injured annually due to preventable errors?

  o 1.3 million due to medication error – U.S. Food and Drug Administration (FDA)[5]

1. Institute of Medicine, www.iom.edu
2. HealthGrades, www.healthgrades.com
3. Agency for Healthcare Research and Quality, www.ahrq.gov
4. Kaiser Family Foundation, www.kff.org
5. U.S. Food and Drug Administration, www.fda.gov
6. *The Journal of the American Medical Association*, jama.ama-assn.org
7. Health Affairs, http://content.healthaffairs.org/content/30/4/596

- 4% to 14% adverse events for all admissions – JAMA 2009[6]

o How much do preventable errors costs annually?

- $17.1 billion – IOM 1999 and Milliman Inc. Study 2011[7]
- $4 billion due to medication errors – IOM 2007

Common Sources of Errors

Sources of errors can be distilled down to two major categories: value stream resources and customers. Medical services are typically delivered with a combination of value stream resources such as people, diagnostic technologies, methods, information technology, medical and operational supplies, equipment, and the environment—any of which can be a source of error. Similarly, customers as active participants in the service delivery process can become sources of error.

Let's take a closer look at typical causes of errors by resource type. Be mindful that sources of error, acting singularly or in combination, may be the cause of one or more defects.

1. People Resources, Including Customers

Unfortunately, human error is an unavoidable and often unpredictable reality. Likely causes of human error are as follows.

- **Lack of Knowledge, Skills, or Ability.** This happens when resources have not received proper training to perform a task and/or their stated capabilities are not verified.

- **Mental Errors.** These include slips and mistakes.

  - **Slips are subconscious actions.** They usually occur when an experienced employee forgets to perform a task.

  - **Mistakes are conscious actions.** They occur when an employee decides to perform a task in a way that results in an error.

- **Sensory Overload.** A person's ability to perceive, recognize, and respond to stimuli is dramatically affected by the sharpness of the five senses. When an employee's senses are bombarded by too many stimuli at once, sensory overload results, and his or her senses are dulled. This increases the chance for error.

- **Mechanical Process Errors.** Some tasks are physically difficult to do and are thus prone to error. They can result in repetitive-strain injuries and physical exhaustion, which are both known to cause errors.

- **Distractions.** There are two types of distractions: internal and external. Both types can lead to errors.

  - Internal distractions include such states of mind as emotional stress and daydreaming.

  - External distractions include high-traffic areas, loud conversations, and ringing phones.

- **Loss of Memory.** Many nonrepetitive work tasks require employees to recall information that can be easily forgotten. Add to this the human factors of aging, drug or alcohol use, and fatigue, which can cause memory loss and lead to unintended errors.

- **Loss of Emotional Control.** Anger, sorrow, jealousy, and fear often work as emotional blinders, hampering employees' ability to work effectively.

2. Diagnostic Technologies

Diagnostic technologies are used to determine the nature and cause of anything (patient condition, equipment failure, and so on). The error caused by diagnostic technologies is misdiagnosis. Diagnostic capabilities rely on accurate measurements and correct interpretations of inputs such as measurements, history, symptoms, and so on. Correct diagnostics also require knowledge of likely or known causes and theoretical problem-solving skills when faced with unfamiliar problems.

Virtually all of the "people" sources of errors can also occur when performing diagnostics. When special equipment and/or measurement devices are used in performing diagnostics, likely sources of errors include out-of-calibration conditions, acuity (accuracy) of measurement, mechanical error, and improper readings or output.

3. Methods

Industry experts believe that most errors occur in the design and execution of tasks—the method for how activities are done. Sources of error in methodologies include the following.

- **Process steps.** Ill-conceived physical and mental steps that resources execute (expected and ad hoc) when performing a service.

○ **Decision making.** This is the process of making a choice among alternatives. Healthcare Enterprises make an incredible number of decisions per day, per month, per year—into the billions. Imagine the opportunities for error!

4. Medical and Operational Supplies

Supplies are the materials we use in the execution of value stream tasks. Common sources of error include using the wrong type or amount, defective supplies (not per specification), improper substitution of one material for another, and incorrect application.

5. Equipment

Equipment errors are created when the equipment does not perform as intended, is incorrectly operated, or is put to unintended use.

6. Environment

Environmental conditions such as poor lighting, excessive heat or cold, and excessive noise levels all have a dramatic effect on human attention, energy levels, and reasoning ability. In addition, unseen organizational influences—such as pressure to perform tasks on time every time, regardless of resource capabilities and availability—can create unhealthy levels of employee competition for recognition and advancement.

Identifying Red-Flag Conditions

The probability that errors will happen is high in certain types of red-flag conditions. Here are a few red flags that should put your error-proofing efforts on full alert.

- **High Variation in Activities.** When a high number of activity variations can be delivered by the same person or the same activity can be performed by a large number of resources.

- **Multiple Resource Requirements.** When an activity requires multiple types of resources (diagnostic technologies, information technology, supplies, special equipment, methods, etc.) at different times and is performed by different resources throughout the delivery process.

- **Activity Specifications Are Rigid and Tightly Controlled.** Deviation from standard of exact process tasks, exactness in sequence, accuracy, acuity, protocols, and so on leads to errors.

- **Multiple Steps.** Most activities involve many small tasks or sub-steps that must be done, often in a pre-set, strict order. If an employee forgets a step, does the steps in an incorrect sequence, or repeats a step, errors occur and defects result.

- **Infrequently Performed Activity.** Infrequent and/or sporadic performance of an activity leads to the increased likelihood that employees will forget proper procedures and methodologies. The risk of error increases when these activities are complex.

- **Lack of an Effective Standard.** Without standards, protocols, and procedures, resources lack insight on expectations and requirements for service performance and outputs. To the contrary, highly complicated or hard-to-understand standards also increase the likelihood of errors.

- **Rapid Repetition.** Activities that are performed quickly, over and over again, increase the opportunity for error. When resources are performing these highly repetitive tasks, the error is often caused by a slip (unconscious mistake).
- **Poor Environmental Conditions.** As stated previously, dim lighting, poor ventilation, inadequate housekeeping, and cluttered workspaces can increase the probability of errors.

How to Error Proof an Activity

Effective error-proofing activities are guided by a structured problem solving approach. A description of the Seven-Step Model is shown below.

1. Describe the problem

2. Describe the current process

3. Identify the root cause(s)

4. Develop a solution and action plan

5. Implement the solution

6. Review and evaluate the results

7. Reflect on learnings

→ Tip: An in-depth discussion of the Seven-Step Problem Solving Model is beyond the scope of this book. For a complete description, please refer to *The Problem Solving Memory Jogger™*.

Use a problem solving model to identify errors, create solutions, and prevent the errors from happening again. During the problem solving process, analyses of activities are performed, sources of errors are discovered, and error-proofing techniques and devices are identified—typically during solution development, and are ultimately validated for effectiveness.

Error Proofing Guiding Principles

It is possible to achieve zero errors by understanding and implementing the four guiding principles of error proofing. These are as follows.

- Apply general inspection techniques
- Achieve 100% inspection
- Use error-proofing devices and data validation rules
- Provide immediate feedback

Guiding Principle #1: Apply General Inspection Techniques

The first, and most important, element of error proofing is inspection. Three types of inspections are commonly used, but they are not equally effective. Ideally one would detect the error at its source, at the exact time of its occurrence, to prevent the defect—this is source inspection. Once the defect has occurred, any subsequent inspection simply informs the activity of its existence. One can only hope that it is caught before the defect makes it way to the next activity or customer—this is informative inspection. The three types of inspection are

1. source inspection;

2. informative inspection; and

3. judgment inspection.

○ **Source Inspection.** Source inspection detects errors in a service process before a defect in the service delivery occurs. The goal of source inspection is to prevent the occurrence of defects by preventing the occurrence of errors.

○ In addition to catching errors, source inspections provide feedback to resources before further processing takes place. Source inspections are often the most challenging element of error proofing to design and implement.

Figure 8-1—Source Inspection

Example: Healing U's ED nurse conducts source inspection by comparing vial color codes by dosage to the amount directed by the attending physician. Even though the nurse reaches for various colored vials, the wrong vials are recognized and placed back into supply and only then is the correct vial taken.

Figure 8-2—Source Inspection Using Color-Coded Vials

o **Informative Inspection.** Informative inspection provides timely information about a defect so that root cause analysis can be conducted and the activity can be adjusted before a significant number of defects occur. Typically, these inspections are done close enough to the time of the occurrence of the defect that action can be taken to prevent further defects from occurring.

The two common types of informative inspections are as follows.

o **Self Inspection.** Resources perform self-inspections at their own workstations or areas. If one finds a defect in an activity, the defect is corrected or discarded. Containment actions are taken to ensure that other defects are not passed on to the next operation or the customer. Subsequently, root cause of the defect is determined and eliminated. Self inspection, as depicted in Figure 8-3, is the second-most-effective type of inspection, behind source inspection. It is much more effective and timely than successive inspection. The number of errors detected depends on the diligence of the service personnel and the difficulty of detecting the defect.

Figure 8-3—Self Inspection

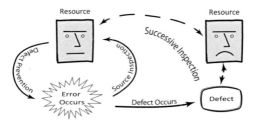

Example: Healing U's ED nurse conducts self inspection and determines that the wrong IV dosage of lidocaine for the patient has been set up—a fortunate catch.

Figure 8-4—Self Inspection of IV Dosage

- o **Successive Inspection.** These inspections are performed after one activity is completed. Employees who perform the next activity in the process perform these inspections. Feedback can be provided as soon as any defects are detected (which is preferable) or simply tracked and reported later.

Figure 8-5—Successive Inspection

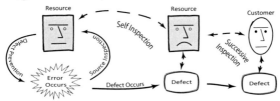

Example: *Healing U's nurse assistant transports a patient to a poorly prepared room. The room inspection sheet had been hastily completed before all bedsheets were properly replaced.*

Figure 8-6—Successive Inspection – Bed Readiness

○ **Judgment Inspection.** We distinguish between two types of judgment inspection: internal and joint. Judgment inspection has two drawbacks. First, it might not prevent the occurrence of multiple defects before final inspection activities, or, even worse, before the customer experiences them. Second, it increases the delay between the time an error occurs and the time a resulting defect is discovered, making root-cause analysis difficult.

  ○ **Internal Judgment inspection.** Often referred to as final inspections, these are inspections during which a healthcare resource compares the final output against a standard or a known customer expectation. If the output does not conform, it is corrected.

Example: Healing U's surgeon discovers that the surgical team left a sponge/gauze inside a patient after abdominal surgery. The metal marker on the sponge was identified during follow-up CT scans after patient complained of pain in his abdomen.

Figure 8-7—Surgical Sponge/Gauze Left Inside Patient

○ **Joint Judgment Inspection.** This inspection occurs during the hand-off with the customer when a defect is discovered, for example, when a healthcare clerk and a patient conduct information verification at time of registration. Wherever practical, empower resources to stop or correct the activity whenever a defect is detected, especially in the customer's presence. Figure 8-8 depicts a healthcare resource and a customer conducting a joint inspection.

Figure 8-8—Joint Judgment Inspection

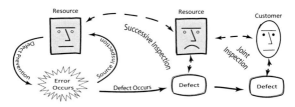

Example: Healing U's registration clerk and the patient conduct a joint judgment inspection when they verify information on the patient's ED wristband.

Figure 8-9—Joint Judgment Inspection of Wristband

Guiding Principle #2: Achieve 100% Inspection

The second element of error proofing is 100% inspection at the time of likely error occurrence. It requires an attitude that "zero defects" is obtainable and rejects sampling as a suitable practice for achieving this goal. Sampling cannot with certainty detect errors or prevent defects from happening or reaching the customer.

At times it may be physically impossible—too time-consuming and costly—to conduct 100% inspection by people. To help achieve zero defects, consider using low-cost error-proofing devices and software rules (see the next section) to perform 100% inspection.

Guiding Principle #3: Use Error-Proofing Devices and Data Validation Rules

The third element of error proofing is the use of devices and data validation rules to make 100% inspection a reality. Physical devices and data validation rules for specific data or field validation enhance or substitute for human senses and judgment. They are designed to improve both the cost and reliability of your organization's inspection activities.

Earlier we stated that services are typically delivered with a combination of resources, including people, information technology, equipment, instructions, materials, tools, and so on. We stated further that any resource can be a source of error. Industry technology providers continue to develop remarkable solutions for detecting and preventing errors. Two principle technologies are useful in the service environment.

○ Physical devices that exploit mechanical, electrical, pneumatic, or hydraulic technology to sense, signal, or prevent existing or potential error conditions created by service resources. Physical sensing devices can detect object characteristics by using both contact and noncontact methods. Contact sensors include microswitches and limit switches; noncontact methods include transmitting and reflecting photoelectric switches.

○ Data validation rules that use metadata (data about data) for data or field authentication. Examples include a data field that requires a number versus text or catches the mistype of "werd" and corrects it to "word" or "weird" based on user preference.

By using physical devices or data validation rules, you can achieve 100% inspection of errors in a cost-effective manner. These physical devices may or may not be combined with software applications.

Common physical error-proofing devices include the following.

○ Physical constraints (walls, barriers, pathways, and so on) of different sizes that physically limit the movement of people and service resources during the service process.

- Physical cues that inform service personnel of proper use of resources or conduct of an activity.

- Alarms or warnings that a service provider activates when he or she detects an error.

- Sensors and other location devices that show the presence and/or absence of service providers, the associated resources (materials, equipment, tools, and so on), or their improper position.

- Counters, devices used to count the number of service tasks performed, resources required or used, and so on.

- Checklists, which are written or graphical reminders of tasks, materials, events, and so on.

Common data validation rules for information include the following.

- Data and field validation rules that sense the presence and quality of data typically found in software applications. Examples include phone number formats, alphanumeric fields for addresses, length of descriptions, required entry (no blanks), and so on.

- Data transmission validation rules that sense the presence, quality of data, and its sequence as it flows between software applications. Examples include making data unable to process due to a missing PIN (personal identification number) or a source that is not authenticated.

- Data workflow validation rules that sense the flow of data according to predetermined work processes. An example is a predefined workflow for a purchase request that does not allow a purchase order to be created unless approved in the correct sequence based on levels of authority.

Setting the Error Through Setting Functions

Such physical sensing devices and data validation rules are the most versatile error-proofing tools available for work processes. When setting up your error-proofing device or technique, be mindful of the practical ways in which errors can be detected. These are typically based on one or more of four unique characteristics.

- **1. Physical Characteristics.** Error-proofing techniques verify size, shape, or color to determine if any abnormalities exist. For example, kitting templates that use cutouts or shape outlines to assure that the right medical supplies and instruments are available to perform a desired procedure.

- **2. Number of Occurrences.** Error-proofing techniques inspect for a specific number of items, events, and so on to determine if any abnormalities exist. For example, a smart IV pump monitor that is used to ensure the correct medication is administered over a desired period of time.

Figure 8-10—Smart IV Pump

- **3. Sequence.** Error-proofing techniques inspect sequence of actions to determine if they are performed out of order. For example, a mobile device or manual check sheet records the sequence in which steps are taken to ensure compliance with a medical protocol.

○ **4. Information.** Error-proofing techniques inspect for accuracy, completeness, and flow of information to authenticate and determine if any errors exist. For example, a business rule establishes that department supervisors can approve purchase requests of up to $500. The purchasing information technology verifies that the requester is indeed the department supervisor and validates the purchase amount before converting the request to a purchase order.

Guiding Principle #4: Provide Immediate Feedback

The fourth element of error proofing is immediate feedback once an error or defect has been detected.

The ideal response is to immediately correct the error or contain the defect. Error-proofing devices and techniques help us achieve this ideal response by providing an immediate warning or taking control of an activity. Let's review.

Warnings

Warnings do not stop an activity; they provide feedback requiring other resources to do so. Common warnings include flashing lights or unusual sounds designed to capture the employee's attention.

Example: A resource types "werd," and the word processing program immediately underlines it with a wavy red line. The person can continue to type but knows that the error has occurred and can fix it before it becomes a defect.

Example: The power is lost to the mobile media cart used during the conduct of medical procedures, and *the battery backup emits a signal indicating its status. The mobile cart continues to operate, even though the principle source of power has been interrupted. In this case the cause of the defect still needs to be corrected.*

Controls

Automatically taking control of an activity is preferred to responding to error conditions, especially when the error has critical consequences to the customer or the service provider. However, it can also be a more frustrating method for the resource if an activity is continually halted because of the error.

Example: *The mistyped "werd" changes automatically to "word" per user preferences. The person can continue to type, unaware that he or she misspelled "word." However, "werd" was supposed to be "weird." The user may have to turn off this autocorrect feature if this is an automatic correction error.*

Example: *The automated protocol stops the surgical preparation process when a conflict in the "right-left" patient information contained on the wristband is inconsistent with the surgeon's physical markings on the patient.*

NINE

Quick Changeover

What Is Quick Changeover?

Quick changeover is a structured methodology for reducing the setup time for an activity. Setup is defined as the preparatory tasks required before an activity can fulfill its intended function.

What Does It Do?

Quick changeover methods focus on reducing resource delays at the start, during, and transitioning between activities that require the changing of resources, of any type.

Why Use It?

Demand for healthcare services is highly dynamic, requiring the quick transition from one type or variant of service to another. Quick changeover methods provide the healthcare provider insight on how to reduce wait times for both the customers and internal resources. Here are a few benefits of applying quick changeover to your processes.

- Reduce the number of labor hours to perform activity setup.
- Reduce the amount, and thus the waste, of materials required for the activity.
- Increase resource capacity associated to a specific activity.
- Reduce setup errors by incorporating standards.

The seven steps of the changeover process are depicted in Figure 9-1.

Applying the Quick Changeover Methodology

Quick Changeover - Seven Step Process

1. Evaluate Current Processes
2. Document Current Changeover Practices
3. Identify Internal & External Activities
4. Shift Internal Activities to External
5. Streamline the Process
6. Evaluate Results of Changes
7. Implement Quick Changeover Activities

Figure 9-1—Quick Changeover Process

This section will review these steps in more detail using a Healing U example. For purposes of illustration, times used for the ED Room Turnover have been exaggerated. Clearly when urgency is heightened the 60 minutes illustrated becomes two minutes in real life.

1. Evaluate Your Current Processes

o Use the Value Stream Map to identify activities that require routine changeover of resources.

o Rank changeover opportunities where improvements in setup or turnover time would positively impact areas such as resource utilization, capacity, safety, health, and cost.

o Use the Data Collection Sheet depicted in Figure 9-2 to record the following.

o Information Collected By

o Process Name/Number

o Setup/Changeover Time Estimate

o Resources/Materials Required

Figure 9-2—Healing U's Data Collection Sheet – ED Patient Room Setup

DATA COLLECTION SHEET

Activity: ED Patient Room Turnover   QCO Team: L. Smith, S. Jordan, M. Shaban

Information Collected by	Process Name	Setup Time Estimate (min.)	Resources	Materials Required
L. Smith	Cleanup Room	30	Third-Party Service Provider	PPE, Cleaning Materials & Equipment
S. Jordan	Makeup Room	20	Third-Party Service Provider	Linen, Pillows
M. Shaban	Restock Supplies	15	Nurse Assistant	Medical Supplies (Various)

2. Document Current Changeover Practices

Use the Data Collection Diagram depicted in Figure 9-3 to record and quantify the following.

o Activity steps beginning at preparation, through use, and cleanup and follow-up

o The cycle time it takes for each activity

o The elapsed time at each step

o General comments regarding resource capabilities, availability, capacity, etc. that impact the activity's cycle

Example: *Healing U evaluates its current process for setting up an ED patient room.*

Additional Documentation Techniques to Consider

o **More Data.** You may desire to bolster your case for change by analyzing and recording the following kinds of information. The capacity typically lost during changeover (turnover) activities, including number of typical services not performed, number of hours that personnel are not engaged in other useful activities, lost service time, and rework (measured in hours and units).

o **Workplace Visualization.** A video recorder is an excellent way to capture your existing changeover practices. It enables employees to review the procedure as many times as needed to fully understand all the steps involved.

o **Identify Waste.** Classify activities as value-adding and non-value-adding. Attempt to eliminate non-value-adding-activities as part of your efforts to improve changeover practices.

Figure 9-3—Healing U's ED Patient Room Setup

QUICK CHANGEOVER DATA SHEET

Activity: ED Patient Room Turnover

Step	Act Type[1]	Element	Time (min.)
10	CR	Put on Personal Protective Equipment (PPE)	1
20	CR	Remove Clutter	3
30	MR	Relocate Chairs	1
40	MR	Place Bed	1
50	MR	Put Clean Linens on Bed	5
60	CR	Scrub Surfaces	20
70	CR	Remove General Trash	2
80	CR	Remove Medical Trash	2
90	MR	Place Portable Equipment	1
100	RS	Stock Medical Supplies	10
110	MR	Place Emergency Cart	1
120	RS	Verify Oxygen Supplies	3
130	RS	Restock Necessities	10

Note 1: CR- Cleanup Room, MR- Makeup Room,

QUICK CHANGEOVER DATA SHEET

QCO Team: L. Smith, S. Jordan, M. Shaban

Elapsed Time (min.)	Notes
1	PPE supplies not located nearby
4	Hand carry to central location
5	No standard for location
6	No standard for location
11	Linen supplies not restocked on a regular basis
31	Cleaning fluid spills are readily evident
33	Hand carry to central location
35	Hand carry to central location
36	No standard for location
46	No standard for replenishment
47	No standard for location
50	No standard for replenishment
60	No standard for replenishment

RS- Restock Supplies

Figure 9-4—Healing U's Internal/External/Waste Chart – ED Patient Room Changeover

INTERNAL/EXTERNAL/WASTE CHART

Activity: ED Patient Room Turnover

Step	Element	Time (min.)	Elapsed Time (min.)
10	Put on Personal Protective Equipment (PPE)	1	1
20	Remove Clutter	3	4
30	Relocate Chairs	1	5
40	Place Bed	1	6
50	Put Clean Linens on Bed	5	11
60	Scrub Surfaces	20	31
70	Remove General Trash	2	33
80	Remove Medical Trash	2	35
90	Place Portable Equipment	1	36
100	Stock Medical Supplies	10	46
110	Place Emergency Cart	1	47
120	Verify Oxygen Supplies	3	50
130	Restock Necessities	10	60

INTERNAL/EXTERNAL/WASTE CHART

QCO Team: L. Smith, S. Jordan, M. Shaban

| Activity Type | | Notes |
Internal	External	
✓		Extra time spent going back and forth to PPE storage
✓		
✓		
✓		
✓		Stock-outs in linen inventory
✓		
✓		No recycling conducted
✓		
✓		
✓		Stock-outs in medical supplies inventory
✓		Ongoing failure to recharge batteries
✓		
✓		Excess supplies held in patient room

3. Identify Internal and External Activities

Use an Internal/External/Waste Chart to record whether an activity is internal or external.

- *Internal activities* are performed while the process is idle (i.e., no customer is being serviced.)

- *External activities* are performed while the process is being engaged (i.e., the customer is being serviced.)

The Quick Changeover Team discovered that none of the activities were performed while the patient was in the room.

4. Shift Internal Activities to External

Using the Internal to External Activity Chart, complete the following steps.

- Identify the activities that employees can perform (concurrently) while they are waiting for other service activities to be completed.

- Identify ways to prepare in advance any resources that must be in place while the service is being performed (e.g., staging resources, gathering supplies).

- Standardize resources that are required for the changeover process, including the following.

  - Information templates and formats

  - Technology and tools

  - Work methods

Figure 9-5 on the next page is Healing U's Changeover Team's recommendations for conducting a portion of activities while the patient is still in the room.

5. Streamline the Process

During this step evaluate whether processes can be streamlined using methodologies discussed in Chapter 5, Continuous Flow. In all cases apply both visual management and error-proofing techniques as described in earlier chapters. Here are a few more suggestions for streaming a process.

Consider ways to eliminate unnecessary delays in your internal activities by

- identifying the activities that can be done concurrently by multiple employees;

- using signals, such as electronic reminders, buzzers, colored lights/signs, and so on to cue employees; and

- simplifying and minifying any physical movements.

Consider ways to eliminate unnecessary delays in your external activities by making improvements in the following areas.

- Storage and transportation of materials, special equipment, and tools

- Leveraging automation

- Increased accessibility of resources

- Creation of a new process map that will be used to guide future activities.

INTERNAL TO EXTERNAL

Activity: ED Patient Room Turnover

Step	Element	Time (min.)	Elapsed Time (min.)
10	Put on Personal Protective Equipment (PPE)	.5	.5
20	Remove Clutter	2	2.5
30	Relocate Chairs	.25	2.75
40	Place Bed	.25	3
50	Put Clean Linens on Bed	3	6
60	Scrub Surfaces	10	16
70	Remove General Trash	.5	16.5
80	Remove Medical Trash	1	17.5
90	Place Portable Equipment	.25	17.75
100	Stock Medical Supplies	1	18.75
110	Place Emergency Cart	.25	19
120	Verify Oxygen Supplies	1	20
130	Restock Necessities	2	22

Figure 9-5—Healing U's Internal to External Activity Chart

ACTIVITY CHART

QCO Team: L. Smith, S. Jordan, M. Shaban

Activity Type		Internal to External
Internal	External	
✓		
✓	✓	Remove clutter throughout the patient stay
✓		
✓		
✓		
✓		
✓	✓	Remove trash throughout the patient stay; add recycling bins
✓	✓	Remove trash throughout the patient stay; add recycling bins
✓		
✓	✓	Set up Kanban 2-bin restocking system; restock throughout patient stay
✓		
✓	✓	Create automated checklist; restock throughout patient stay
✓	✓	Set up Kanban 2-bin restocking system; restock throughout patient stay

Activity: ED Patient Room Turnover

Step	Element	Time (min.)	Elapsed Time (min.)
10	Put on Personal Protective Equipment (PPE)	.5	.5
20	Remove Clutter	2	2.5
30	Relocate Chairs	.25	2.75
40	Place Bed	.25	3
50	Put Clean Linens on Bed	3	6
60	Scrub Surfaces	10	16
70	Remove General Trash	.5	16.5
80	Remove Medical Trash	1	17.5
90	Place Portable Equipment	.25	17.75
100	Stock Medical Supplies	1	18.75
110	Place Emergency Cart	.25	19
120	Verify Oxygen Supplies	1	20
130	Restock Necessities	2	22

Figure 9-6 is Healing U's Future State – Streamlined Process Chart. Improved practices were recommended for every activity.

STREAMLINED PROCESS

QCO Team: L. Smith, S. Jordan, M. Shaban

Activity Type		Improvement
Internal	External	
✓		Create PPE local stocking location
	✓	Remove clutter throughout the patient stay
	✓	Mark floor; relocate chair while patient in room
✓		Mark floor
✓		Set up Kanban 2-bin restocking system
✓		Create standardized cleaning protocol
	✓	Remove trash throughout the patient stay; add recycling bins
	✓	Remove trash throughout the patient stay; add recycling bins
✓		Mark floor
✓	✓	Set up Kanban 2-bin restocking system; restock throughout patient stay
✓		Mark floor; add sign to plug in cart
✓	✓	Create automated checklist; restock throughout patient stay
✓	✓	Set up Kanban 2-bin restocking system; restock throughout patient stay

6. Evaluate Results of Changes

It is time to conduct a trial run or two to test and validate your proposed changes. Take a close look at the results of the changes you have made. Do the results match your improvement estimates? If not, make the necessary adjustments or consider other ways in which you can streamline your changeover activities and make the process external.

Figure 9-7 reveals Healing U's validated streamlined process results. The resultant changeover time of 22 minutes represents a 63% reduction in overall time, improving the overall patient room capacity by nearly 25%, given current patient length of stay in the ED.

7. Implement Quick Changeover Activities

Now that you have proven the process, it is time to reap the benefits. Before you close the project file make sure you

o document the new procedures and train all involved employees on the new procedures;

o create and/or revise lean documents such as Value Stream Maps and Process Flow Diagrams; and

o continue to collect data for continuous improvement of the changeover process.

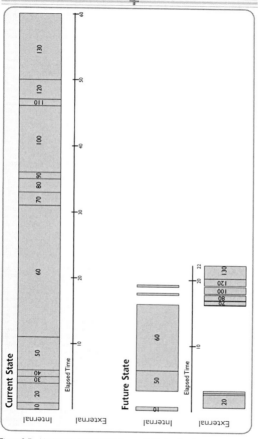

Figure 9-7—Healing U's Future State Process Validation Results

Chapter

THE KANBAN SYSTEM

What Is a Kanban System?

The Kanban system is a methodology that uses cards or other physical devices as visual signals for triggering or controlling the flow of supplies (medical supplies, special equipment and devices, spare parts, administrative materials, etc.) during the order fulfillment process. It synchronizes the logistic processes within the Healthcare Enterprise and between the Healthcare Enterprise and outside suppliers.

What Does It Do?

In the Kanban system, a card (referred to as a Kanban) controls the movement of items between supply locations and points of use. When an activity needs supply items, it sends the corresponding Kanban to the supply source; the card acts as the item requisition or pseudo purchase order. A Kanban card contains the following data.

- What is needed
- When it is needed
- How much to deliver
- How to transport it
- Where to store it

Why Use It?

In an ideal world, demand for supplies would be constant. Thus supply chains would always operate at maximum efficiency, delivering exactly what is needed—no more, no less. However, for the Healthcare Enterprise, the need for supplies can vary considerably by the minute, hour, day, week, or month.

The goal of the Kanban system is to balance the risk of not having the right supplies at the right time against the cost of carrying excess supply inventory that might not be consumed during the desired time period or might never be consumed. The Kanban system fine-tunes your supply replenishment processes to deliver on a constant order quantity or constant order cycle basis. It is not designed to quickly respond to sudden large spikes in demand.

Where to Start

Before you can put the Kanban system in place, you must first understand the nature of demand for the supplies you require. This involves conducting an analysis of consumption, such as maximum usage, frequency of usage, typical usage quantity per event, and so on, ultimately distilling this information into a required quantity per day/week/month. This information will assist in determining the appropriate number of Kanbans to use.

The Three-Bin System for Healthcare

For a Healthcare Enterprise, a three-bin system is perhaps the most useful model for the Kanban system. A three-bin system, as depicted in Figure 10-1, consists of one bin at the Point of Use (POU). The second bin is held in the central store within the Healthcare Enterprise. The third bin is held at the supplier's store.

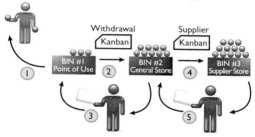

Figure 10-1—Three-Bin System

In the three-bin system Step 1 occurs when an end user withdraws supply items from the POU Bin #1. Step 2 occurs when Bin #1 becomes empty and a withdrawal Kanban is carried to or collected by the central store. Step 3 occurs when the central store replenishes the POU bin from its stock. Step 4 occurs when stock levels hit a minimum safety level and a supplier Kanban (material requisition) is issued. Step

5 is the subsequent supplier delivery of a predetermined amount of supply items.

Kanban Guidelines

When using the Kanban system, it's important to follow the six general guidelines listed below.

1. An upstream source never sends defective supply items to a downstream process.

- Supply resources must have a system in place to prevent errors or to discover a defective item prior to issue or shipment.

- The problem(s) that created the defective supply item or incorrect order delivery must be resolved immediately.

- All defective items mixed with good items must be separated promptly.

- Suppliers who ship defective items to your organization must send the same number of replacement items in their next shipment. This ensures that the exact number of good items required is available to conduct healthcare services.

2. A downstream process withdraws only what it needs from inventory.

- No withdrawal of supply items from storage is allowed without a Kanban.

- Withdraw the same number of items as Kanbans (unless a Kanban indicates item quantities of 1 +).

- A Kanban must accompany each item.

3. Upstream sources deliver the exact quantity of supply items that will be withdrawn by the next process downstream.

o Inventory must be restricted to an absolute minimum. This is called just-in-time inventory (see the next section).

o Do not supply more items than the number of Kanbans (unless a Kanban indicates item quantities of more than one).

o Supply items in the order in which their withdrawal Kanbans are received.

4. Synchronize your supply processes by regularly evaluating delivery schedules and reassigning resources as needed.

5. Remember that the Kanban system is a way of fine-tuning your delivery amounts.

o The Kanban system cannot easily respond to major changes in demand requirements.

o Use advance planning and communication processes for unusual demands.

6. Work to stabilize and improve your supply processes. Highly variable and erratic work methods often result in poor delivery performance. Make sure you keep all your work processes in control and aligned to the changing requirements of your customers.

How Many Kanbans Should I Use?

The number of Kanbans you should use depends on the type of inventory-control system you have. There are two types: the constant order-quantity system and the constant order-cycle system.

With a *Constant Order-Quantity* system, a downstream process orders a predetermined, fixed quantity of supply items from an upstream process whenever inventory levels drop to a predetermined reorder point. This is the quantity level that automatically triggers a new order. Because the order quantity is fixed, the reorder date varies.

A *Constant Order-Cycle* system, on the other hand, features a fixed reorder date and a varying order quantity. The quantity of supply items ordered depends on the number of items used since the previous order was placed.

Both types of inventory-control systems have pros and cons. Because the number of Kanbans used in a *Constant Order-Quantity* system always stays the same, this type of system makes it easy to error proof your delivery processes for these constant, known quantities. Also, it is easy to apply visual management techniques to reflect constant stock levels and use of storage space. However, using a *Constant Order-Quantity* system increases the complexity of coordinating the movement of supply items throughout your healthcare facility.

A *Constant Order-Cycle* system, on the other hand, reduces the complexity of coordinating the movement of supplied items throughout your healthcare facility. This makes this type of system ideal for healthcare systems that use externally supplied items, where coordinating fixed restocking of stores or inbound freight is critical. However, using a *Constant Order-Cycle* system increases the complexity of managing the number of Kanbans in the system because of variable production quantities within a fixed time period. Error proofing and visual management techniques are also more difficult to use when supply quantities vary significantly.

The fewer Kanbans you have, the better. Having too many Kanbans means you have too much planned inventory. You should monitor and adjust your Kanban levels so that you order only the minimum amount of inventory required to enable end-user departments to meet their demand. Too many Kanbans, just like excess inventory, can hide problems.

Constant Order-Quantity System: Reorder Point Calculation

Reorder point:

average usage during lead time + safety stock – orders placed but not yet received

Total number of Kanbans:

$$\frac{\text{economic lot size} + (\text{daily demand} \times \text{safety coefficient}}{\text{container capacity}}$$

Or:

$$\frac{\frac{\text{monthly demand}}{\text{monthly number of setups}} + (\text{daily demand} \times \text{safety coefficient})}{\text{container capacity}}$$

Constant Order-Cycle System: Maximum Inventory Calculation

Maximum inventory:

daily demand × (order cycle + lead time) + safety stock

where the order cycle is the time interval between an order time and the next order time, and the lead time is simply the time interval between placing an order and receiving delivery.

Order cycle:

$$\frac{\text{economic lot size for an expected demand}}{\text{daily average demand}}$$

Economic lot size:

$$(Q) = \sqrt{\frac{2AR}{ic}}$$

where
A = ordering cost per lot
R = monthly estimated demand quantity
i = carrying cost per dollar of an item; and
c = unit cost

Order quantity:

(standard quantity - existing inventory) - (orders placed but not yet received)

Total number of Kanbans:

$$\frac{\text{daily demand} \times (\text{order cycle} + \text{lead time} + \text{safety period})}{\text{container capacity}}$$

where lead time = processing time + waiting time + conveyance time + Kanban collecting time

More detailed explanations for these equations are available from many industry sources, including *Toyota Production Systems: An Integrated Approach to Just-In-Time*, Third Edition, by Yashiro Monden (Engineering and Management Press, 1998).

ELEVEN

TOTAL PRODUCTIVE MAINTENANCE

What Is Total Productive Maintenance?

Total Productive Maintenance (TPM) is a series of methods which ensures that every piece of equipment, regardless of where it is used, always performs as designed at the time of need. In essence, TPM is healthcare for equipment.

What Does It Do?

TPM is a team-based approach that continually enhances normal equipment monitoring and maintenance activities, resulting in improved equipment performance, availability, and reliability.

Why Use It?

Equipment performance is essential to the core capabilities of all Healthcare Enterprises. The most vital pieces of equipment are those associated with the Healing Pathway.

By working together under a structured TPM methodology, equipment users and maintenance resources improve equipment health, resulting in

o improved performance;

o increased availability;

o improved quality output;

o increased reliability;

o increased life;

o improved equipment usage; and

o increased patient and user safety.

How Do I Implement TPM?

Implementing TPM involves the following five steps.

1. Improve Overall Equipment Effectiveness (OEE) of vital equipment

2. Establish and implement autonomous maintenance

3. Create a planned maintenance program

4. Establish an equipment life-cycle management program

5. Plan for and conduct continuous-improvement activities

These five steps are described in detail on the following pages.

Step 1: Improve Overall Equipment Effectiveness (OEE) of Vital Equipment

The goal of your TPM program is to maintain, restore as necessary, and improve equipment health, with a focus on the vital equipment that impacts both the Healing Pathway and operations. The *Overall Equipment Effectiveness* (OEE) metric ensures that equipment health is being sustained. OEE measures three aspects of equipment performance: *Availability, Performance Efficiency,* and *Quality Throughput.*

Establish a baseline OEE, where OEE = |Availability % x Performance Efficiency % x Quality Throughput %| for individual pieces of equipment. Set a benchmark of 85% OEE for each piece of equipment. The OEE goal is usually not 100% because this would leave no time for planned maintenance or for purposefully choosing to operate a piece of equipment at less than its design rate.

Motivate resources to maintain and improve equipment health by monitoring and reporting equipment-related losses. The following seven types of equipment loss are useful ones to track.

1. Downtime due to equipment failure

2. Time required for setup and adjustments (positioning, priming, powering up, cleaning, etc.)

3. Time or cycles lost to inefficient setup (locating, sequence of startup, etc.)

4. Time or cycles lost to special attachment performance (changeable components of the equipment that touch the patient or the work product)

5. Time or cycles lost to unavailable operator or user (missing equipment user, loss of power, etc.)

6. Operating at less-than-ideal speeds (reduced throughput, longer cycle times, etc.)

7. Producing defective throughputs that require rework

Be wary of unintended consequences of improving one OEE variable by worsening another. For instance, don't increase equipment *Performance Efficiency* if it results in defective throughput. Also, where practical, correlate your OEE with your company's financial indicators. An improvement in OEE can then be expressed in terms of reduced costs or additional revenue.

Example: *Healing U compares its OEE to the benchmark*

Healing U deploys an Inhalation Anesthesia Machine for use in operating, induction, and recovery rooms. It can be used with O_2, N_2O, and air supplied by a medical gas pipeline system or by externally mounted gas cylinders.

> Availability for Use = 85%
>
> First Time Through Quality (FTT) = 99%
>
> Performance Efficiency = 99%

$$OEE = 85\% \times 99\% \times 99\% = 83\%$$

This OEE of 83% does not quite meet the benchmark of 85%.

Step 2: Establish and Implement Autonomous Maintenance

In autonomous maintenance, equipment users are trained to assume routine inspection and adjustment tasks so that they can share the responsibility for the care of their equipment with the maintenance staff. When equipment users perform the routine tasks of maintenance, such as checking, adjusting, and lubricating equipment, maintenance technicians are then free to focus on more complex repairs and problem-solving activities to eliminate future breakdowns.

Seven Elements of Autonomous Maintenance

Autonomous maintenance involves seven elements. They are outlined in Table 11-1.

Table 11-1—Seven Elements of Autonomous Maintenance

The Seven Elements of Autonomous Maintenance

Element	Purpose
1. Initial Cleaning	• Reduces contamination • Increases user's familiarity with equipment and work area • Uncovers hidden defects
2. Preventive Cleaning Measures	• Identifies, isolates, and controls sources of contamination, including leaks, process-related excess, and materials from the external environment
3. Development of Cleaning and Lubrication Standards	• Combines inspections for cleanliness with lubrication checks so that they can both be performed as efficiently as possible
4. General Inspection	• Conducts torquing, adjustments, and minor calibrations • Inspects hydraulic, pneumatic, and electrical subsystems
5. Autonomous Inspection	• Equipment users assume responsibility for lubrication, cleaning, and general inspection of their equipment • Users must also be trained on the technical aspects of the equipment

6. Process Discipline	• Improves methods and procedures to foster efficiency and repeatability, benefits include
	  - reduced setup times;
	  - decreased activity cycle times; and
	  - standardized procedures for handling equipment and part requirements.

7. Independent Autonomous Maintenance	• Self-sustaining improvement

Before You Begin

Before you begin your autonomous maintenance activities, ask the following questions.

Is our equipment's performance, availability, or throughput quality significantly affected by one or more of the following?

o Workplace contamination

o Loose connectors or fittings

o Loose screws and bolts

o Lack of lubrication

2. Is our workplace made unsafe by one or more of the following?

o Workplace contamination

o Fluid leaks

o Exposed or damaged equipment components

Are there any routine, low-skill maintenance procedures that equipment users can perform that would also serve one of the following purposes?

o Enhance the user's sense of ownership over the quality of the area and the work

o Minimize equipment downtime

o Extend equipment life

Do equipment users and maintenance technicians have a good working relationship? Will the implementation of autonomous maintenance strengthen that relationship?

o Those times during which there are no pressing equipment problems and there is a lull in activities are good opportunities for maintenance technicians to thoroughly review equipment use and care with the users. This helps build proactive, positive relationships among coworkers. For more ideas about building cooperation and teamwork, consult *The Team Memory Jogger*™.

Basic Training of Equipment Users

Start your autonomous maintenance program by providing equipment users basic technical, troubleshooting, and problem-solving training; this can be done by maintenance staff or equipment manufacturers. Some important tips to teach equipment users are listed below.

- Use only proper cleaning solutions and devices. Using improper chemicals can degrade product quality and/or corrode your equipment. Using incorrect cleaning tools can scratch or damage equipment.

- Eliminate unacceptable equipment vibration. Excessive vibration can be an indicator of bearing failure, loose mounts, or bolts.

- Identify any worn or broken components. Equipment users can often easily recognize worn tooling, broken meters, broken gauges, nonfunctioning sensors, and loose belts.

- Eliminate all sources of contamination. Foreign materials, such as dust, foodstuffs, or packaging materials, can quickly wear out your equipment. Preventing contamination helps to prolong equipment life.

Step 3: Create a Planned Maintenance Program

The term *planned maintenance* refers to maintenance activities that are performed per a predefined schedule. The goal of a planned maintenance program is to reduce the amount of *reactive maintenance*, which is maintenance activities that are performed after a piece of equipment breaks down. Understanding that, in the equipment health world, "stuff happens," the goal is to understand why equipment fails, determine if failure can be predicted, and then determine when the optimal maintenance action needs to be taken. Consider the following when setting up your planned maintenance program.

Maintenance Types

The four types of maintenance actions:

Maintenance Types	
Maintenance Type	Description
Reactive	Responding to breakdowns
Preventive	Periodic checking, adjusting, and replacing of parts to prevent future equipment failures
Predictive	Forecasting potential problems by measuring process variables and the condition of the equipment, then adjusting and replacing parts to prevent future equipment failures based on this forecast
Maintenance Prevention	Improving equipment design to eliminate the need for maintenance

Equipment Designs Matter

Your equipment's design determines most of its maintenance requirements. Many Healthcare Enterprises work with their equipment suppliers to design equipment that requires fewer and less-complicated maintenance procedures. Design engineers can reduce the amount of required maintenance by placing an emphasis on component durability, reliability, and ease of service.

Computerized Maintenance Management Systems (CMMS) Are a Must

TPM programs are most successful in healthcare enterprises that use a computerized maintenance management system (CMMS) to support potentially hundreds of pieces of equipment with thousands of parts and supplies required to support them. Below is an outline of the basic elements of a CMMS.

1. A work identification system that
   - specifies the problem (e.g., a needed repair on a piece of equipment);
   - identifies the location of the problem;
   - identifies the likely cause of failure; and
   - assigns a priority to the problem.

2. A work authorization system that
   - prioritizes all work requests based on the nature of the demand;
   - eliminates duplicate requests;
   - decides which work can be safely postponed; and
   - turns approved repairs into work orders that are planned, scheduled, and executed.

3. A work management system for the maintenance department that
   - identifies the equipment or area that needs work;
   - establishes communication with the person who requested the work;
   - diagnoses the problem;
   - orders the needed parts and materials; and
   - schedules a time for the repair to take place.

4. A preventive maintenance system that
   - schedules and performs periodic checks on equipment, lubrication, and the replacement of worn parts;
   - triggers inspection, adjustment, repair, and replacement work orders;
   - tracks compliance with the maintenance schedules; and
   - correlates preventive maintenance activities with equipment reliability and availability.

5. An equipment history system that records the entire performance/repair history of all critical equipment.

6. A cost reporting system that records all costs related to equipment maintenance, including hidden costs caused by
   - poor maintenance;
   - downtime;
   - defective throughput; and
   - negative customer impact.

Step 4: Establish an Equipment Life-Cycle Management Program

An equipment life-cycle management program maximizes the return on your company's equipment investment. Such a program has seven phases as outlined in Figure 11-1.

Equipment Lifecycle Management Considerations

Here are a few practical thought-starters to help improve your equipment lifecycle management activities.

o Treat the seven equipment life-cycle phases as an integrated system, much like a value stream. Lean improvement methodologies apply throughout each phase, just as they do for a value stream.

o Do not accept equipment failure as a *fait accompli*. Use the OEE to drive improvements in design, use, maintenance, and upgrade activities—with the ultimate objective of eliminating or preventing all critical failures.

o Recognize spare parts for what they are—stock waiting for something to fail before it has value. Use spare parts consumption data to drive equipment reliability efforts.

o Do not become a hoarder of spare parts and used equipment; doing so ties up valuable cash resources of the Healthcare Enterprise.

Figure 11-1—Healing U's Equipment Lifecycle

The Equipment Lifecycle

The Equipment Lifecycle phases represent the logical flow of activities for the planning through disposal of physical (tangible) assets. The lifecycle phases apply to all market segments and uses for equipment.

Evaluation & Planning	Phase 1 - Evaluation & Planning activities detail how the equipment owner assesses equipment use, performance, and capacity requirements against existing and future operational requirements.
Organize & Standardize	Phase 2 - Organize & Standardize activities detail how standalone and integrated equipment are combined to perform required functions, assign organizational responsibility, and, where practical, apply standards.
Design & Build	Phase 3 - Design & Build activities describe industry activities to design equipment to general market or customer specific functional, reliability, and serviceability requirements. Similarly build this equipment to design specifications.
Acquire & Install	Phase 4 - Acquire & Install activities detail how the equipment owner acquires equipment to its requirements, installs equipment, and releases equipment for use by the organization.
Maintain & Repair	Phase 5 - Maintain & Repair activities guide how the organization takes stewardship of the equipment, continually evaluates, maintains, and repairs equipment to performance requirements.
Overhaul & Upgrade	Phase 6 - Overhaul & Upgrade activities detail how an organization plans for and conducts significant equipment restoration and repair activities, or upgrades the equipment in whole or in part to meet existing or new functional requirements.
Divest & Dispose	Phase 7 - Divest & Dispose activities guide organizational activities to evaluate the remaining useful life of an equipment for continued uses, other organizational uses, market resale, or disposal.

Step 5: Plan For and Conduct Continuous Improvement Activities

Equipment users, maintenance resources, engineering staff, and supervisory personnel should all take an active role in planning your company's continuous improvement initiatives for equipment. These initiatives can include autonomous maintenance, planned preventive maintenance, and asset management (i.e., all activities and tasks performed throughout the asset life cycle).

Once your continuous improvement plans are in place for both your existing and new equipment needs, individuals and teams should conduct directed activities and report on their progress. These plans should be integrated into your company-wide lean initiatives and Total Quality Management (TQM) activities.

Figure 11-2—Healing U's Equipment Lifecycle Capabilities Assessment

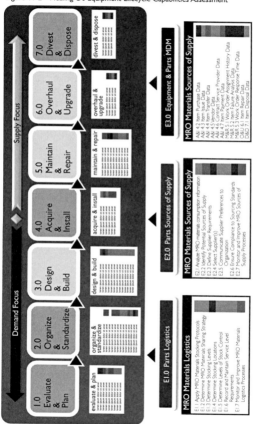

Example: Healing U starts a TPM program

After completion of high-level evaluation of its Equipment Lifecycle Management capabilities, as depicted in Figure 11-2 on the previous page, Healing U was able to quickly identify weakness in its maintenance capabilities—ultimately guiding its continuous improvement activities. A team was assembled to initiate a TPM program for all mobile equipment used principally in its operating room and EDs, given both the significant number of users and their impact on patient care.

Using the three dimensions of OEE, members of the team began categorizing the various problems they are having with their mobile equipment. The *Inhalation Anesthesia Machine* is used as an example.

Availability

Healing U's Inhalation Anesthesia Machine suffers intermittent failure affecting an average of three surgical procedures per week. Most of these failures are overcome through jiggling the Vapor Interlock System switch out of the middle double-locked position. Figure 11-3 is a simplified diagram of the interlock mechanism.

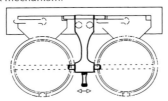

Figure 11.3—Inhalation Anesthesia Machine – Vapor Interlock System

First Time Through Quality (FTT)

When the interlock system fails, sometimes all vapor flow stops; other times, vapor appears to be leaking. The flow rate does not appear to be affected when this occurs.

Performance Efficiency

Upon closer inspection, when the interlock position is correct the performance of the Inhalation Anesthesia Machine is as designed.

Applying the Seven TPM Elements

Healing U's team applies the TPM process steps to the Inhalation Anesthesia Machine as follows.

Initial Cleaning

Healing U owns 20 Inhalation Anesthesia Machines from two original equipment manufacturers (OEM). The suppliers of the machines were requested to conduct a cleaning and inspection workshop for users (nurses and nurse assistants) and the lead technician for mobile OR equipment. During the initial cleaning activities, a physical inventory of both the mobile equipment and vapor canisters was taken. It was found that certain machines are used more often than others and show visible signs of wear and tear.

Preventive Cleaning Measures

The Healing U team found that it is possible to confuse and thus mix OEM vapor canisters between the two types of Inhalation Anesthesia Machines. This was further evidenced by opened packages and containers of vaporizers that had not been returned to stock. When conducting inventory, the team found that when these canisters are stocked, they are grouped by vapor content only and not separated by OEM. The slight differences in OEM designs lead to improper sealing at installation—often resulting in force fitting canisters, which prevents the correct operation of the locking mechanism.

Development of Cleaning Standards

Based on the results of their initial cleaning and preventive cleaning measures, the Healing U team decided to produce OEM identifier labels that match the canisters to the correct Inhalation Anesthesia Machine. They placed bright labels on each machine warning users, "Do not Force Fit Canisters into Position!"

General Inspection

The Healing U team developed visual aids that provided instruction for the correct fit-up of canisters and visual examples of damage points created by force fitting incorrect canisters.

Autonomous Inspections

With the new instructions in hand, all users were trained on proper procedures for canister fit-up and locking. Equipment users received further cleaning instructions and guidance on how to properly disposition incorrect canisters.

Process Discipline

The Healing U team developed metrics to enable equipment users to monitor and report the Inhalation Anesthesia Machine's performance. This metric becomes the basis for a recognition system for the team that does the best job of improving the Inhalation Anesthesia Machine's OEE.

Independent Autonomous Maintenance

Today, each OR team appoints a lead nurse and nurse assistant who receive additional training about Inhalation Anesthesia Machine diagnostics and maintenance. These leads attend a quarterly feedback and problem-solving meeting about Inhalation Anesthesia Machine problems.

Healing U's Inhalation Anesthesia Machine problems soon begin to disappear.

Daily maintenance activities are performed as expected, and Inhalation Anesthesia Machine users are now able to conduct more difficult diagnostics on their own. Given its success, Healing U continues to apply TPM methods to other critical healthcare equipment.

The Lean Memory Jogger™ for Healthcare | ©2012 GOAL/QPC

TWELVE

STANDARD OPERATIONS

What Are Standard Operations?

The term *standard operation* refers to the most efficient utilization of resources through the design and execution of Healing and Business Pathway activities. An activity is comprised of resources, methods, and protocols that enable a desired capability.

- **Resources** include people, methods, protocols, materials, facilities, special equipment, tools, information technology, and so on that come together to enable the completion of an activity.

- **Methods** are procedures, plans of action, ways or manners in which one conducts business, techniques, and systematic arrangements of actions that guide the work process.

- **Protocols** are rules that guide decision making within a method.

What Do They Do?

When you apply all your knowledge of lean principles to a particular Healing or Business Pathway (value stream) activity to make it as efficient as possible, a standard operation is the result. Resources then use this standard operation as the guideline for completion of all activity tasks.

Why Use Them?

It is the optimal lean combination of resources, methods, and protocols that enables the delivery of healthcare services at the highest possible value and lowest possible operational cost.

Putting together standard operations forces you to break down each of your work processes into definable elements. Each element is analyzed for resource requirements, timing expectations, core actions, and decision-making protocols. This analysis enables you to readily identify waste, solve problems, and provide all resources with guidance about the best way to get things done.

How Do I Develop Standard Operations for My Organization?

The process for developing standard operations involves nine steps. The output of one step is used as input by the next (e.g., value stream mapping, to service blueprinting, to demand queuing strategies, to continuous flow, and so on). The nine steps are as follows.

1. Establish standard operations team(s).

2. Determine activity service level objectives.

3. Determine the exact task sequence.

4. Determine activity lead time.

5. Determine activity process capacity.

6. Determine the standard quantity of work product and materials.

7. Prepare a standard workflow diagram.

8. Prepare a Standard Operations Sheet.

9. Continuously improve the standard operation.

The remainder of this chapter discusses these nine steps in detail.

Step 1: Establish Standard Operations Team(s)

Standard operations teams are typically formed as part of a *Lean Transformation*. Given the importance of establishing and institutionalizing standard operations, experience suggests that a team-based approach is best. Lean organizations understand the need for buy-in and support of all resultant changes and compliance to standardized activities.

Step 2: Determine Activity Service Level Objectives

Begin creation or modification of standard operations by defining service level requirements the activity must achieve. Service level measures the performance of a system in meeting customer demand at the time and place required (e.g., 85% of patients entering the ED are examined within 15 minutes of arrival). Over time, value stream activities exhibit an average level of performance (mean) as well as its variability (standard deviation). Your goal should be to achieve desired service levels within a given level of variation. The following are examples.

- All calls are answered on average by three rings, plus or minus one ring.

- All ED patients requiring admissions wait on average 45 minutes before being placed in a hospital room.

- All medical supply orders will be filled 95% of the time on the same day, 98% by next day. Backorders to be filled within five working days.

Normally service levels are balanced against the investment in resources required to achieve them. For example, a 95% service level may require too many resources that sit idly until an expected large demand occurs. In this case the organization may find that an 85% service level is cost-effective and does not cause undue customer waiting and dissatisfaction. Here are a few more tips for establishing an effective service level.

Use the P_cQ Analysis

To help determine the right service levels, perform a P_cQ analysis (Ch. 6) to help you determine customer demand rates and frequency.

Calculate Takt Time

With P_cQ analysis results in hand, calculate takt time as a general guide to process lead time and capacity design decisions (where takt time is the customer demand rate). Takt time enables your organization to balance the pace of its activities to match the rate of customer demand. The mathematical formula for determining your takt time is as follows.

$$\text{Takt time} = \frac{\text{Available daily service time (ie., hours of operation)}}{\text{Required daily quantity of output (ie., customer demand)}}$$

Establish the Hours of Operation

The hours of operation is the amount of time resources are made available to deliver a healthcare service. In this case, takt time is simply the hours of operations divided by the customer demand rate. In the service world, where demand is often sporadic and the lead times for supply are shortened, takt time is the broadest of estimate of how often supply of services needs to occur to meet an average demand level over a defined period of time. Be mindful that different service processes and offerings may have different demand rates at different times of the day (inside and outside your service window) and thus different takt times.

Consider Shift Work Impact on Performance

Healthcare enterprises make people-dependent services available through shift design. This helps establish and manage customer expectations for service.

Example: Healing U, like many Healthcare Enterprises, is under considerable pressure. Given increases in demand and scarce resources, it has adopted 12-hour shifts—requiring nurses specializing in surgery, dialysis, and ICU to be available on call around the clock. But, because humans aren't machines, there are certain factors to consider when designing shift work. Here are a few important ones. (Source: "Shift Work, Safety and Productivity," *Occupational Machine* 2003; 53:95–1–1, Folkard, S., Tucker, P.)

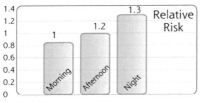

Figure 12-1—Relative Risk Across Shifts

Because people are circadian, meaning their biological processes recur naturally on a twenty-four-hour cycle, afternoon and night shifts work counter to this natural clock and thus increase risk in the workplace.

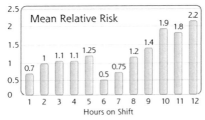

Figure 12-2—Relative Risk – Length of Shift

Risk varies across the length of the shift. As many work places move to four 10-hour days, it is interesting to note that the risk factors nearly double in hour 10. In sum, the longer we work, the higher the risk factors. Unfortunately service level requirements usually don't get easier over the course of a shift.

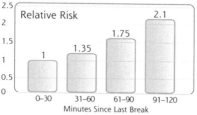

Figure 12.3—Relative Risk – Minutes Since Last Break

Looking at the relative risk between breaks shows that once again sustained efforts without mental or physical breaks increase risk of poor performance. This risk is so real that many governments have enacted meal and break laws that impact shift design.

Step 3: Determine the Exact Task Sequence

Task sequence is the order in which value stream activities are performed. Task sequence provides resources with the correct order in which to perform their duties. A Standard Operations Combination Chart (SOCC) enables your standard operations team to study the work sequence, associated lead times, periods of waiting, and other lean wastes. In such a chart, each task is listed sequentially and broken down into manual, automated, wait (batch or process delays), and walk times.

Figure 12-4—Healing U's EC Standard Operations Combination Chart (SOCC)

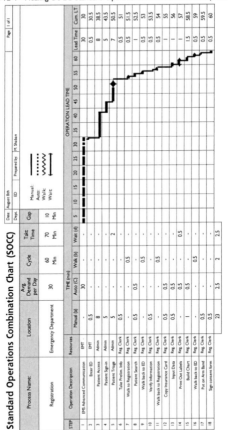

Completing the SOCC

The steps for completing a standard operations combination chart are described below.

o At the top of form in Figure 12-4, indicates the following.
  o Date that the work process is being mapped
  o Number of pages (if the chart is more than one page long)
  o Department where activity is performed
  o Name of the preparer
  o Name of the process or activity being mapped
  o Location where the activity is performed
  o Average demand per a defined time period
  o Total cycle time
  o Takt time
  o Gap defined as the difference between the takt time and the cycle time

o The block labeled "Time" indicates the type of units in which the work activity is usually measured. Activities are normally measured in seconds, but some are measured in minutes or even longer intervals.

o If the takt time is less than the cycle time, draw a line that represents the activity's takt time. Trace the line with red so it stands out.

o Sequentially number each operational step in the appropriate column. Steps can include any or all of the following.

- Manual operations
- Automated operations
- Time spent walking from one location to another
- Time spent waiting
- Provide a brief name and description for each step.
- Note the time required for the completion of each step in the appropriate column.
  - Draw a horizontal line on the graph representing each step, using the following guidelines.
  - The length of the line should equal the duration of the step.
  - The line type should match the action type (see the line key at the top of the sample chart).
  - Each line type should be in a different color, which will make your chart much easier to read.
- Each line you draw should begin at the point on the vertical time-line that corresponds to the actual time the activity begins. It should end at the actual time the activity ends.
- Indicate lead time for each process step.
- Indicate cumulative lead time as cross check to horizontal lines.

Interpreting the SOCC

Your completed SOCC should provide you with some useful insights, including the following.

- If the total time to complete the process or activity

equals the red takt-time line, congratulations! You already have an efficient work combination in place.

○ If the total time to complete the process or activity falls short of the red takt-time line, you might be able to add other operations to the activity to use your resources more effectively.

○ If the total time to complete the process or activity is longer than the red takt-time line, the process as designed will not consistently meet customer expectations.

Use the following steps to identify where this waste occurs.

○ Look for ways to compress cycle times or eliminate process steps altogether.

○ Look for opportunities to conduct parallel activities when a resource is waiting for automated tasks to be completed.

○ Look for ways to minimize movement of resources. Can you reduce or eliminate any of it by relocating supplies or equipment or rearranging workspaces?

Step 4: Determine Activity Lead Time

Lead time is the time it takes to successfully complete the tasks required for a work process. It is important to note that a work process's lead time may or may not equal its takt time. Lead time can be broken down into three basic components.

1. **Cycle time.** This is the time it takes to complete the tasks required for a single work process, such as

performing equipment maintenance or completing patient registration.

2. **Batch delay.** This is the time a task waits while other tasks are completed or processed. An example is the time the first patient registration document must wait until multiple patient registration documents are completed and entered into the system at one time.

3. **Process delay.** This is the time that batches of tasks must wait after one activity ends until the next one begins. Continuing the batch delay example, a process delay occurs between the time patient registration information is entered and the time the registration clerk prints out the patient's wristband.

Lead time analysis can be conducted as part of your value stream mapping activities or at the completion of the SOCC.

Step 5: Determine Activity Process Capacity

Determine your process capacity before making any significant changes to activities. Compare lead time to takt time to determine if process capacity must be changed to meet demand requirements. Use the Process Capacity Table as depicted in Figure 12-5 to gather information about the activity and the time required to complete each task. This information will ultimately be used to determine resource capacity requirements.

Figure 12-5—Healing U's EC Process Capacity Table

Process Capability Table

Date 3/1 Page 1 of 1   Prepared by: M. Shabani

Type	Process Name:	Net Operating Time/Shift (G)	# of Shifts	Max. Out. Per shift (H)	Req. Out. Per shift	Takt Time (min)	
	Service Delivery Process:	2100	3	8	6	70 Min	
				Processing Time			
STEP	Operation Description	Resources	Manual (A)	Walk (B)	Auto (C)	Total Cycle (D) (D=A+B+C)	Serv. Capacity per shift G/D
1	EMS Advanced Communication	EMT	-	-	30	30	
2	Enter ED	EMT	0.5	-	-	0.5	
	Activities Subtotal		0.5		30	30.5	23
3	Patient Access	Admin	8	-	-	8	
4	Patient Sign-in	Admin	5	-	-	5	
5	Patient Triage	Admin	5	-	-	5	
	Activities Subtotal		18			18	39
6	Take Prelim. Info	Reg. Clerk	0.5	-	-	0.5	
7	Walk to Registration	Reg. Clerk	-	0.5	-	0.5	
8	Patient Search	Reg. Clerk	0.5	-	0.5	1	
9	Walk Back to ED	Reg. Clerk	-	0.5	-	0.5	
10	Verify Information	Reg. Clerk	0.5	-	-	0.5	
11	Walk back to Registration	Reg. Clerk	-	0.5	-	0.5	
12	Copy Insurance Card	Reg. Clerk	0.5	-	0.5	1	
13	Input Data	Reg. Clerk	0.5	-	0.5	1	
14	Print Out Labels	Reg. Clerk	-	-	0.5	0.5	
15	Build Chart	Reg. Clerk	1	-	0.5	1.5	
16	Walk Back to ED	Reg. Clerk	-	0.5	-	0.5	
17	Put on Arm Band	Reg. Clerk	0.5	-	-	0.5	
18	Sign Consent Form	Reg. Clerk	0.5	-	-	0.5	
	Activities Subtotal		4.5	2	2.5	9	78
	Activities Total		23	2	32.5	2.5	12

Steps for Creating a Process Capacity Table

1. Enter date.

2. Enter number of pages (if the chart is more than one page long).

3. Enter name of preparer.

4. Enter the process name.

5. Record the net operating time per shift.

6. Enter the number of shifts.

7. Calculate the maximum output per shift derived from capacity table.

8. Enter the sequence number of each processing step being performed.

9. Create subtotal lines for grouped activities.

10. Record the operation description, which is the activity being performed.

11. Enter the classification or description of the resource performing the activity.

12. Record the walk time, the approximate time required between the end of one process and the beginning of the next process.

13. Enter the manual time, the time an employee must take to manually perform service activities when an automated activity is not being performed. The manual time includes any known batch or process delays.

14. Record the automated time, the time required for a machine's automatic cycle to perform an operation, from the point when the Start button is activated to the point when the finished part is ready to be unloaded.

15. Calculate the total cycle time by adding the manual time and the automated time.

16. Subtotal cycle times by natural groupings of activities.

17. Enter the service capacity per shift (also known as the total capacity). This is the total number of activities that can be performed during the available hours per shift or per day.

18. Record the takt time for the work process in the takt time box, using the mathematical formula shown earlier in this chapter.

19. Calculate the total capacity of the process by adding all activity subtotal times and dividing the sum by the net operating time/shift.

Step 6: Determine the Standard Quantity of Work Product and Materials

The standard quantity of resources is the minimum amount of work product or materials to be held at or between your work areas. Without having this quantity of completed work on hand, it is impossible to synchronize your work operations. Review Chapter 10, The Kanban System, for insight on how much work product and/or materials should be held. When determining the best standard quantity of resources you should have, consider the following points.

- Try to keep the quantity as small as possible.

- Ensure that the quantity you choose is suitable to cover the time required for performing the service.

- Make sure that the quantity enables all employees to easily and safely handle the movement of resources like equipment, tools, materials, and so on between service activities.

Step 7: Prepare a Standard Workflow Diagram

A standard workflow diagram shows your organization's current area and equipment layout. It also depicts the movement of employees and resources during service processes. Such a diagram helps your lean improvement team plan future improvements to your organization, such as continuous flow (Ch. 6).

The workflow diagram as depicted in Figure 12-6 provides a visual map of workspace organization, movement of materials and workers, and distances traveled—information not included in either the Process Capacity Table or the SOCC. You can use this information to improve your workspace organization, resequence your work steps, and reposition your equipment, materials, and workers to shorten your cycle time and overall travel distance. This will help you to achieve your takt time.

The information in your workflow diagram supplements the information in your Process Capacity Table and SOCC. When combined, the data in these three resources serves as a good basis for developing your standard operations sheet (see Step 8).

Figure 12-6—Healing U's Standard Current State Workflow Diagram

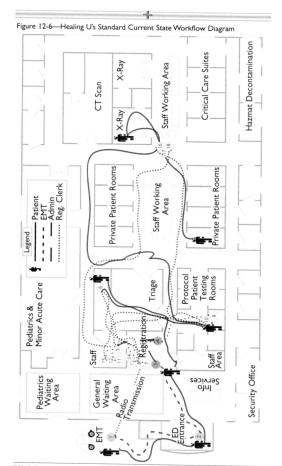

Steps for Completing a Standard Workflow Diagram

1. On the diagram, indicate the following.

   The name of the activity being mapped.

   The date the activity is being mapped.

   The name of the person completing the diagram.

   The revision level if multiple revisions are expected.

2. Sketch the work location for the work process you are mapping, showing the typical resources (equipment, tools, storage, materials, and so on) used in the activity.

3. Indicate the work sequence by numbering the activities by location in the order they occur.

4. Connect the activity numbers with solid lines, starting with 1 and continuing to the highest number needed.

Step 8: Prepare a Standard Operations Sheet

The Standard Operations Sheet combines information from the Process Capacity Table, SOCC, and the workflow diagram into one process standard. It depicts the beginning, the current state, and the future state intentions of your lean efforts over a period of time in a single diagram. Figure 12-7 shows the Healing U Standard Operations Sheet at the beginning of Healing U's lean journey.

Figure 12-7—Healing U's Current State Standard Operations Sheet for Patient Registration

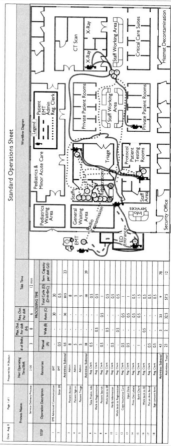

©2012 GOAL/QPC

Step 9: Continuously Improve the Standard Operation

After you complete your Standard Operations Sheet, you should train all resources who are affected by your changes on the work process in question. Don't be surprised if, during this training, they discover potential opportunities for even greater improvement.

It is through the continuous improvement of your standard operations that your organization can systematically eliminate waste and reduce costs. You should review your organization's standard operations sheet(s) on a periodic basis to ensure accuracy and resource compliance.

THIRTEEN

LEAN METRICS

What Are Lean Metrics?

Lean metrics are defined as a system or standard of measurement that is used to gauge progress towards the six lean goals of defining demand, extending demand lead time, matching supply to demand, eliminating waste, reducing supply lead time, and ultimately reducing total costs. Lean metrics are often part of a larger analytics initiative, where analytics is defined as the extensive use of data (statistical and quantitative), explanatory and predictive models, and fact-based management to drive decisions and actions.

What Do They Do?

Lean metrics help your Healthcare Enterprise measure its progress toward its lean goals and objectives. When applied to the Healing Pathway and other value streams, they encourage prioritized and integrated improvement efforts.

Why Use Them?

Lean metrics serve to focus, prioritize, and unify the organization's improvement efforts at achieving customer satisfaction (quality, cost, and delivery), matching supply to demand, reducing waste, and reducing lead time. When combined in an integrated analytics system, an organization can systematically monitor and drive performance improvement efforts.

Analytics Categories

- Effectiveness
- Efficiency
- Cycle Time
- Integration
- Costs

Customer

Internal Processes

Financial

Learning & Development

Lean analytics can be classified into four data management categories described by the Balanced Scorecard. The Balanced Scorecard as introduced by Robert Kaplan and David Norton is designed as a performance planning and measurement framework. When combined with Lean and Six Sigma initiatives, the Balance Scorecard methodology helps focus the organization on things that matter to the success of the company.

o **Customer.** Does the organization deliver products and services to the satisfaction of the customer?

o **Internal Processes.** Are internal processes lean and effective in matching supply to demand?

o **Learning and Development.** Are motivated and trained employees applying the right skills required to deliver products and services or to perform internal processes as required?

o **Financial.** Has the company invested wisely in its offerings (marketing, design, development, and delivery) as well as in the resources (people, facilities, equipment, materials, information technology, and so on) of the organization?

This memory jogger provides examples of customer and internal process metrics. However the goal question metric (GCM) methodology (discussion follows) can be applied to each balanced scorecard category. Further, enterprise mapping (Ch. 2) enables you to map all processes, including financial and learning and development, and their associated metrics.

The Goal Question Metric Approach

The Goal Question Metric (GQM) approach is an excellent method by which a lean organization can frame and ultimately identify and select its lean metrics. This methodology was designed in a cooperative effort by Victor Basili, Gianluigi Calderia, and H. Deiter Rombach. The GQM methodology begins as the organization describes its goals. It asks pertinent questions regarding goal accomplishment and, from these questions, metrics become apparent.

Goal-*Driven Lean Metrics*

Lean metrics tend to be very specific to the six integrated lean goals (Ch. 1). In keeping with the GQM method, the six lean goals should guide metrics development.

1. Define Demand for Services

2. Extend Demand Lead Time

3. Match Supply to Demand

4. Eliminate Waste

5. Reduce Supply Lead Time

6. Reduce Total Costs

Questions *that Lead to Lean Metrics*

The second step of the GQM method is to ask pertinent questions that provide information about goal accomplishment. The identification and ultimate deployment of the right metric can be a daunting task without this rational approach. So what questions should be asked? Industry has generically classified the types of questions that we can use to derive lean metrics. These core questions include:

○ **Effectiveness.** Did we produce the desired or intended result? Did we match supply to demand? Did we achieve customer satisfaction? Were business objectives reached?

- **Efficiency.** Did we use resources as designed without wasted time or effort?

- **Cycle Time.** Did we execute tasks in the order and time frame as designed?

- **Integration.** Did outputs from one activity necessarily become the input to the next activity?

- **Total Cost.** How much money was invested, required, or given in payment for something?

Metrics *Data Collection Template*

It may be helpful to develop a data collection template that ensures that the metric's identification, development, and deployment are successful. Consider the use of the following metrics development template to help define and integrate metrics into an overall analytics process.

Lean Metric Template

Metric Description	Describe the Metric
Lean goal supported	Determine the lean goals to which the metric will be applied. Define Demand for Services, Extend Demand Lead Time, Match Supply to Demand, Eliminate Waste, Reduce Supply Lead Time, Reduce Total Costs
Analytic category	Indicate which of the four Balanced Scorecard categories applied: Customer, Internal Process, Financial, and Learning and Development
Question classification	Indicate which of the five questions you are attempting to answer: Effectiveness, Efficiency, Cycle Time, Integration, or Total Cost
Why was it selected?	Describe the specific purpose of the metric
Who will be using the metric?	Identify who or what will be interpreting and using the metric
When and where will the data be obtained?	Describe the time and, where appropriate, the location at which data will be collected
How will the data be collected?	Describe the mechanics of the data-collection process
What formula(s) will be used for calculation(s)?	Detail the equation(s) to be used
Sample calculation	Show sample calculations
How often will it be calculated?	Describe the frequency of the metric
How often will the metric be used?	Define how often interpretation of the metric will be conducted and used by the organization

The Basics of Data Collection

The Goal Question Metric (GQM) helps us derive information by comparing metrics to goals. Let's say we want to define metrics for achieving the third lean goal of matching supply to demand. We need to dig a bit deeper and consider the fundamentals of the data collection.

o *What is the purpose of the data we are collecting?* Are we meeting customer demands at the time of need?

o *Will the data tell us what we need to know?* By collecting the wrong data and/or untimely data, we may not be able to determine the effectiveness in matching supply to demand. For example, do we measure demand as if it only occurs during normal office hours (like 8:00 A.M. to 4:30 P.M.) or does demand more likely occur during off hours?

o *Will we be able to act on the data we collect?* Even if we gather the right data, did we apply the right analysis techniques to help us interpret it correctly and guide our decisions? For example, if enough demand occurs during off hours, is it sufficient enough to justify changes in office hours, changes in staffing to accommodate off-hour support, and so on?

Designing a Data-Collection Process

When you design your data-collection process, keep the following points in mind.

o Make sure that all employees who will collect the data are involved in the design of your data-collection process.

- Use the Lean Metric Template to explain how the data will be used.

- Ensure that employees understand that the main driver for data collection is process improvement, not finger-pointing.

- Design data-collection forms (hardcopy or online) to be user friendly.

- When developing a data-collection procedure, describe how much data is to be collected, when the data is to be collected, who will collect the data, and how the data is to be recorded.

- Automate data collection and charting whenever possible.

- Involve employees in the interpretation of the data.

Avoid the following pitfalls.

- **Measuring everything.** Focus instead on the few critical measures that can verify performance levels and guide your improvement efforts.

- **Misinterpreting data.** Show employees why and how the data was captured. Also tell how the data will be used in your lean enterprise initiative.

- **Collecting unused data.** Data collection is time consuming. Ensure that all the data you collect will be put to good use.

- **Communicating performance data inappropriately.** Avoid creating harmful fault finding, public humiliation, or overzealous competition.

Remember to use the appropriate tools for your analysis. Less-experienced teams can use basic tools such as Pareto Charts, Histograms, Run Charts, Scatter Diagrams, and Control Charts. Refer to *The Memory Jogger*™ 2 for insight on the purpose and use of each of these tools.

Lean Metrics Examples

Numerous metrics that are effectively deployed in a lean initiative. Using the GQM method will help you identify and select metrics that make sense. Here are a few examples of common lean metrics that healthcare organizations find useful.

- **Service Level:** Leaving Without Being Seen

- **Process Lead Time:** ED Patient Waiting Time

- **First Time Through Quality:** Medical Diagnosis

- **On-Time Delivery:** Medical Supplies

Service Level measures the ability of a system to meet demand as requested by the customer. As demand-related goals are defined, the service level gives the percentage to which they should be achieved.

Process Lead Time is the average time that elapses during the completion of defined healthcare activities. Process lead times consists of task cycle times, batch delays, and process delays. The goal for Healing U in using this metric is to identify and reduce patient wait times in the ED. It is believed that by reducing wait times, the number of patients leaving without being seen (LWBS) will be positively impacted, as will hospital revenues.

Healing U - Lean Metric Template

Metric description	Service Level—Leaving Without Being Seen (LWBS)
Lean goal supported	Match Supply to Demand—Ability to serve all who arrive at the ED.
Analytic category	Customer
Question classification	Effectiveness
Why was it selected?	To determine if customer demand for emergency medical care is being met
Who will be using the metric?	Emergency Department
When and where will the data be obtained?	At the time customer arrives and departs from the ED
How will the data be collected?	Healing U's EDIS (Information System)
What formula(s) will be used for calculation(s)?	% of patients LWBS by point of departure

Sample calculation	Total Patients 1,000	#	%
	Left the waiting room	60	6%
	Before registration	7	.7%
	Before triage	8	.8%
	Before seeing a physician	20	2%
	Before final disposition	6	.6%
	Total LWBS	101	10.1%

How often will it be calculated?	Daily
How often will the metric be used?	Summary statistics developed daily, weekly, and monthly by ED triage type & point of departure

Healing - Lean Metric Template

Metric description	ED Patient Wait Time
Lean goal supported	Reduce Supply Lead Time
Analytic category	Customer, Internal Process
Question classification	Efficiency
Why was it selected?	To determine if ED processes are performed timely, with no wasted effort or delays, and in the correct sequence to achieve ideal process lead times
Who will be using the metric?	ED, Hospital Leadership
When and where will the data be obtained?	At various points in the ED treatment process
How will the data be collected?	Through automated time stamping in Healing U's EDIS (Information System)
What formula(s) will be used for calculation(s)?	Start-Stop actual & approximate times captured in system

Sample calculation

Patient Event	Start	Stop	Wait Time
ED Entry	0800		
Recognized	0810	0803	10
Wait Area	0803	0833	30
Triage	0833	0835	
Exam Room	0835	0845	10
Examined	0845	0852	
Exam Room	0852	0900	8
Treated	0900	0915	
Exam Room	0915	0930	15
Dispositioned	0930	0945	
Total	105 min	Wait Total	73 min (69.5%)

How often will it be calculated?	Per Event
How often will the metric be used?	Summary statistics developed daily, weekly, and monthly by service type and location

First Time Through Quality is the percentage of medical diagnostics that are performed without defect. How frequently do doctors misdiagnose patients? In a Supplement to the May 2008 issue of the *American Journal of Medicine*, a collection of articles and commentaries sheds light on the causes underlying misdiagnoses and demonstrates a nontrivial rate of diagnostic error that ranges from <5% in the perceptual specialties (pathology, radiology, dermatology) up to 10% to 15% in many other fields. There are no quick fixes, according to the Agency for Healthcare Research and Quality (AHRQ).

On-Time Delivery is the percentage of medical and operating supplies that are delivered per the customer's timing expectation. The goal is to reduce the number of stock-outs of critical care items. The question of whether the facility is stocking the right quantities in the right locations needs to be answered.

Healing - Lean Metric Template

Metric description	First Time Through Quality (FTTQ)
Lean goal supported	Define Demand - Correct Diagnosis of Patients
Analytic category	Customer, Internal Process, Learning & Development
Question classification	Effectiveness, Efficiency
Why was it selected?	26% of Healing U's medical malpractice claims are for diagnosis errors. These claims are driving up legal and insurance costs.
Who uses metric?	ED staff
When and where will the data be obtained?	Direct feedback from customer, autopsy evaluation, Board reviews of diagnoses
How's data collected?	Healing U's Medical Records System
What formula(s) will be used for calculation(s)?	% of misdiagnosis at varying diagnostic stages: access/presentation, history taking/collection, physical examination, testing, assessment, referral, and follow-up

Sample calculation

Diagnostic Process	What went wrong	#	%
Ordering	Failure/Delay in ordering needed tests	2	.2%
	Failure/Delay in performing ordered tests		
	Suboptimal test sequence	1	.1%
Performance	Sample mix-up/mislabeled (e.g., wrong patient)	1	.1%
	Technical errors/poor processing of specimen/test	2	.2%
	Erroneous lab/radiol reading of test	3	.3%
Clinician Processing	Failed/delayed follow-up action on test result	1	.1%
	Erroneous clinician interpretation of test		
Total Diag. 1000	Total—what went wrong	10	1%

Excerpted from Diagnosis Error Worksheet

How often will it be calculated?	Per Event
How often will the metric be used?	Summary statistics developed daily, weekly, and monthly by service type and location

Healing U – Lean Metric Template

Metric Description	On-Time Delivery
Lean goal supported	Match Supply to Demand - Material Stocking Levels Match Demand
Analytic category	Internal Processes
Question classification	Effectiveness
Why was it selected?	ED complaining of too many stock-outs and back orders for critical supplies, e.g., EKG Pads
Who will be using the metric?	Procurement and ED
When and where will the data be obtained?	Request date and quantity captured in Healing U's ERP system; storeroom log indicating stock-out
How will the data be collected?	Healing U ERP System: MM Module
What formula(s) will be used for calculation(s)?	% of complete orders delivered per request date (not vendor promise date)
Sample calculation	OTD_{EKG} = 3 lines delivered per request date ÷ 4 total line ordered x 100 = 75%
How often will it be calculated?	Instantaneous per delivery receipt
How often will the metric be used?	Summary statistics developed daily, weekly, and monthly by order type, part type, and shipping location

Lean Human Capital

> Every time you walk into a hospital or clinic in the United States, you take your life in your own hands. Whatever your condition, you will probably be cared for by people who are overworked and hobbled by wasteful systems.
>
> — Toussaint & Gerard, On the Mend

Only you can judge whether Toussaint & Gerard are more right than wrong as it applies to your organization. What we can state with certainty is that *lean is not the healing process; it is the process for healing processes.* And in so doing, breathing life back into the healthcare resources whose very actions impact the lives of those they serve.

Throughout this text we have introduced multiple lean tenets that impact the role and performance of the healthcare associate. For example:

Multi-skilled workforce – as a consideration for achieving continuous flow (Ch. 6)

People as common sources of error (Ch. 8)

Shift work impact on performance (Ch. 12)

Any serious Lean Transformation effort will impact people's lives. This impact is a worthy discussion and the purpose of this appendix. We hope to challenge and enlighten your thinking in the following discussion topics.

- o Challenging the Lean Costs Reduction Primacy
- o Lean Goals put Customers and Associates First
- o Lean Respect for People

- Lean Healthcare Requires Human Capital
- Lean Values Human Capital as an Asset
- Lean Values Adaptive Resource Capabilities
- Lean Invests in Human Capital
- Lean Promotes Self-Reliance and Reliance on Others

Challenging the Lean Costs Reduction Primacy

Some suggest that lean considers *people* strictly a… *"Costly, less efficient, and more burdensome" cog in the machinery of production*. And if cost reduction is the principal driver for a Lean Transformation, does this not by definition put people's jobs at risk? The very same "overworked" people asked or directed to engage in the Lean Transformation… to achieve the noble objective of Perfect Care?

Consider survey results from the Lean Enterprise Institute (LEI) released in August of 2007, which found that 46.1% of nearly 2,500 businesspeople surveyed rate "reduced cost" as the greatest benefit of implementing lean management concepts. According to Dave LaHote, LEI "This may explain that while many organizations like the savings they get with a focus on lean tools and waste reduction, few significantly change their competitive position and even fewer break through to lead their industry in quality, value, innovation, growth and profitability, as Toyota has done in the auto business."[1]

Cost first means patients and associates last. Lean heals costly processes, with the highest cost being paid by patients who feel that *"they must take their lives into their own hands."*

Lean Goals put Customers and Associates First

Lest we forget the Lean Goals presented in Chapter 1, have a bigger purpose of achieving *Perfect Care* for patients, not to drive out costs at all cost! Further, the sequence of the Lean Goals have a bigger purpose —to assure that healthcare associates are engaged in meaningful activities, in the right order to secure, not threaten their future. Let's briefly review this sequence, one more time.

Goal 1 – Define Demand puts the patient as the primary focus, not the doctor. **Goal 2 – Extend Demand Lead Time** requires that the organization pay attention to both future patient demand (foresight) and current demand (insight). Customer intimacy gained from Goals 1 and 2, enable the healthcare enterprise to understand what resources (who, what, when, where, why, and how) it requires to achieve **Goal 3 – Match Supply to Demand**. Now the focus shifts to the required resources; capabilities of the doctors, nurses, medical specialists, staff, and so on. **Goal 4 – Eliminate Waste** challenges everyone in the healthcare enterprise to look for value-destroying activities and eliminate them. **Goal 5 – Reduce Supply Lead Times** focuses on achieving improved cycle times and where practical, apply continuous flow of value-creating activities to match supply to demand instantaneously—Just-in-Time (JIT). And finally, not first, not even second, third, fourth or fifth, **Goal 6 – Reduce Total Costs** seeks to optimize the combination of resources (people, technology, facilities, supplies, etc.) necessary to deliver services at a price that both the patient and the healthcare organization can afford.

Lean Respect for People

Lean methods transform work activities, value streams and overall healthcare enterprise capabilities—*people's jobs will be impacted.* Toyota leadership understood this as a necessary outcome of Lean Transformation activities. They expect to invest in *right-sized and multifunctional machines*, arranged in work cells, producing only that which the customers purchased. They had similar expectations for production workers—*right-sized and multi-skilled.*

During a lean transformation, machines do not *feel* threatened with loss of employment, people do. But to Toyota leadership the bigger threat is *waste*, and it makes clear that "respect for human beings means not having them engage in wasteful work or jobs." Not doing so "elevates the value of human being and in turn constitutes respect for them.[1]" Today, Toyota associates continue to understand this philosophy as a hallmark of marketplace success. By cooperatively applying lean they mitigate market risk associated with inefficient and costly manufacturing practice; thus achieving a higher level of job security, now and into the future.

Lean Healthcare Requires Human Capital

Human capital is defined as the person's abilities, knowledge, capacities and qualities of character. To improve *human capital* requires one to invest in *human capabilities*; what I can do, how much I can do, motivation to do it, and how do others experience me when I am doing it or not doing it.

It is nearly impossible to imagine the pursuit of *Perfect Care* without incredibly skilled and talented people. Where certain capabilities are uniquely human; skills of emotional discernment, holistic diagnosis, psychological and physical care, all of which compassionately delivered to those suffering from illness or disease. These are core capabilities of a Lean healthcare enterprise—*human capital* that matters!

Lean Values Human Capital as an Asset

Lean methods focus on defining and characterizing what *resource capabilities* are required to deliver healthcare services first and foremost. Lean methods seek to *objectively* evaluate each resource according to its capabilities; resources like people, technology, special equipment, facilities, etc. Lean methods then seek to *optimally combine* resource capabilities to deliver healthcare services with the ultimate objective of achieving the Lean Perfection Standard.

> —#— Instantaneous satisfaction of a demand, in the form of; time, place, cost, and experience desired by the customer; doing so with the optimal economic combination and sequencing of resources at any given moment in time.

If this lean approach to people appears to be a bit too clinical or antiseptic, consider this. Lean values all value-creating resources as assets. Assets whose *tangible and intangible value* is a function of their capabilities to deliver what is expected by the customer, individually or in combination with other resources.

Lean does not summarily apply classical accounting rules to resources, where the *machine is an asset* and the *person is an expense.* To repeat, lean deems *investment in all value-creating resources as an investment in assets, not an expense.* By doing so lean pays the ultimate respect to the person, especially those who continually invest time and effort to advance their capabilities to the betterment of the customer, themselves, and the organization as a whole.

Conversely, *Lean gets Mean* when healthcare leadership uses lean methods solely to drive cost reductions where associates are classified as expenses—to be cut. When value-creating people are cut, with less capability or unnecessary resources retained, the patient and the healthcare enterprise will undoubtable suffer. This cost-cutting death-spiral is not the intent of lean—never has been and never should be.

Lean Values Adaptive Resource Capabilities

In pursuit of the Lean Perfection Standard, healthcare organizations must be driven to constantly sense and adapt to changes in patient needs, diagnostic methods, treatment protocols, medicines, regulatory requirements, and resource (technology, people, facility, special equipment, etc.) capabilities—all things demand and supply. As healthcare services change, resources of all types may be reclassified as value-destroying, unnecessary, or no longer reflect the optimal combination to deliver *Perfect Care.* This includes *Human Capital!*

A healthcare enterprise actively pursuing lean perfection by default becomes an adaptive organization. Constantly evaluating what resources it needs to "invest in" and "divest of" to advance *Perfect Care* capabilities. However, it is not newsworthy when outdated x-ray machines find new life in a distant country or are repurposed based on their components and material content. In contrast it is newsworthy when an outdated person joins the rank of the unemployed, especially in todays' trying economic times.

At its essence, lean evaluates all resources by their value-creating capabilities. Whereas the x-ray machine is not capable of self-improvement, the person is. The person is also capable of improving other resources, like the x-ray machine, like an associate, like a work process, and so on. It is this *innate human desire and capability to improve all things* that the *Lean Transformation* relies on; that a successful healthcare enterprise must rely on. Thus *Not Utilizing People's Abilities—No Empowerment* has rightfully taken its place as one of the eight lean wastes.

Lean Invests in Human Capital

A lean organization does not leave *human capital* unattended, inevitably to become unproductive, uninspired, and uncommitted to personal and organizational success. It creates and deploys *Lean Transformation Governance* that advances a culture of personal and organizational improvement in constant pursuit of Perfect Care.

The Lean Healthcare Implementer's Field Book, provides useful insight of the establishment of the *Lean Transformation Governance*. It seeks to create a patient-driven (demand), not a physician-centric (supply) organization that applies the Six Lean Goals (Ch. 1), across all healthcare services (demand) and associated Healing and Business Pathways (supply).

The Lean Transformation Governance seeks to break down organizational silos that exist between departments and medical specialties by promoting multi-disciplinary activities to establish clear protocols for prioritizing patient demands (Ch. 5) and to achieve Continuous Flow for the full spectrum of patient services (Ch. 6). The Lean Transformation Governance seeks to enhance dialogue through team-based activities such as Enterprise Mapping (Ch. 2), Value Stream Analysis (Ch. 3) and Service Blueprinting (Ch. 4). It makes acceptable open review of practices as they occur (Gemba) while proactively allaying fears of what might be observed. The Lean Transformation Governance encourages individuals and departments to make immediate and meaningful changes to the work environment through Visual Management Kaizen Events (Ch.7). It seeks to abolish barriers that exist between competing improvement management practices. For example, applying Quick Changeover (Ch. 9) methods as part of a Theory of Constraints (TOC) initiative; applying Error Proofing (Ch. 8) methods as part of Total Quality Management (TQM) patient satisfaction initiative or as the *Improvement*[2] solution in a Six Sigma DMAIC (problem solving) activity.

Accomplishing all of the above requires organizational commitment to ongoing assessment, training and development of people; a real and tangible investment in *human capital*! And collectively, an investment in knowledge management (KM) as healthcare enterprises apply strategies and practices to identify, create, represent, distribute, and enable adoption of insights and experiences of its human capital.

Lean Promotes Self-Reliance and Reliance on Others

My thoughts matter, my opinions matter… I matter. Would everyone in your organization state these words in the affirmative? A self-reliant person would. Why? Because they understand that they own both their capabilities and the decision to engage them. And what capabilities they develop and what decisions they make determine whether they survive, grow, and ultimately engage life in a way that increases their well-being and the well-being of those that matter most to them.

Self-reliance does not imply independence from others. To the contrary, self-reliant people understand that they must contribute their talents to the good of the whole in order to increase the quality of their lives, both personally and professionally. In return, self-reliant people have only one seemingly small requirement—that those they engage life with are also self-reliant. On the whole, healthcare associates are self-reliant. Individually they have invested many hours, if not years of study and practice just to be able to apply their skills; for a cause bigger than themselves—that of serving others.

A successful Lean Transformation depends on people who are self-reliant; where personal aspirations and a desire to serve others to the best of their abilities is not an anomaly, but an expectation. It is these self-reliant resources who will drive the complacent insane, who will challenge thinking and doing at all levels and in all areas. They will work tirelessly for a purpose bigger then themselves. And sadly it is these very same self-reliant people who have been shut-down, discounted, and told to simply do their jobs or risk losing it—by the very same self-reliant people holding positions of leadership.

Through effective Lean Transformation Governance individual dignity is restored, regardless of organizational stature. It does so by empowering associates to identify waste, improve all resource capabilities, to streamline operations, and create standards that hold themselves and others to account.

Abraham Lincoln stated that *"people of equal value, sharing a common vision; will achieve immeasurable success."* *"People of equal value"* requires everyone to be self-reliant such that, *my thoughts, my opinions… I matter* is balanced by respect for others such that, *their thoughts, their opinions… they matter*—and together *we matter!*

Perfect Care must become the *common vision* of all healthcare associates; associates who trust that every individual, team, department, and institution will indeed engage their talents towards this end.

To those who have created and advanced Lean methods we owe a great thanks. For they have provided all of us with a great gift—a humane gift, for enabling individuals and organizations to achieve the *"immeasurable success"* they seek.

---

[1] Learning the ABC's of Economics. (2007, November). Industry Week, 16.

[2] Hino, S. Inside the Minds of Toyota. New York: Productivity Press, 2006. Print.

O

P